Charles W Boase

An Account of the Families of Boase or Bowes,

originally residing at Paul and Madron in Cornwall; and of other families

connected with them by marriage

Charles W Boase

An Account of the Families of Boase or Bowes,
originally residing at Paul and Madron in Cornwall; and of other families connected with them by marriage

ISBN/EAN: 9783337102036

Printed in Europe, USA, Canada, Australia, Japan

Cover: Foto ©ninafisch / pixelio.de

More available books at **www.hansebooks.com**

AN ACCOUNT

OF THE

FAMILIES OF BOASE OR BOWES,

ORIGINALLY RESIDING

AT PAUL AND MADRON

IN

CORNWALL:

AND OF OTHER FAMILIES CONNECTED WITH THEM

BY MARRIAGE, &c.

Privately Printed

(Seventy-five Copies only.)

FOR CHARLES WILLIAM, GEORGE CLEMENT, AND FREDERIC BOASE,
BY WILLIAM POLLARD, PRINTER, NORTH STREET, EXETER.

1876.

PREFACE.

—

The following account of the Boase family and of persons with whom they have been and are connected in marriage is now printed for family use only; and with the twofold object of preserving the information collected by the compilers of this work, and of eliciting from the various heads of families further and more accurate details about their own branches. This must therefore be considered in the light of a preliminary sketch to be filled up more fully on a future occasion.

The difficulties of writing even a short work of this nature will be known to all who have been engaged in similar pursuits; no apology is therefore offered for the occurrence of a certain number of mistakes which were unavoidable, since almost every line contains a fact or a date.

Mr. George Bown Millett of Penzance is now engaged in editing the earliest register of the parish of Madron, a work which will be useful to place beside this family history, as by its use it will be possible to verify many of the dates here mentioned and add further particulars.

The Compilers desire that their relatives will kindly supply an account of errors and omissions, with additional matter respecting intermarriages and the pedigrees of families with which such marriages have taken place.

It is hoped that this work may serve to keep up a feeling of relationship between families now scattered far and wide over Great Britain, but all tracing their original descent to the county of Cornwall.

INDEX.

The letter *p* in *italic* following after a name denotes that the reference is to the folding Pedigree sheet at the commencement of this volume. The figures refer to the columns of the text. It is also to be noted that in this Index all Christian and Surnames are spelt in one way only, notwithstanding the various spellings which are to be found elsewhere, and that as a rule one reference only is given to each page, although the name may occur more than once on the same page.

Robert,bap* 4 Aug.1650=Mary Rawling of Penzance, removed to Penzance, bur.* 6 Aug. 1749. ? after 1705, mar.* 23 Apl. 1705, bur.* 13 Feb.172?

Robert,bap.†26 Feb. 170?,bur.*27Sept. 1708, "son of Robert of Penzance."

Arthur of Tredavo,=Florence dau. of bap.* 1 Nov. 1652, mar.* 18 June 1686, bur.* 5 Oct. 1731. | ander Martack, 30 Sep. 1658, die fore her husband

---

Charity, mar.*=John Trewavas 15 April 1710, of Paul, ? bur.* bur.* 17 March 28 Jan. 1778. 1777.

Anne, bap.* 11 =Bernard Yeaman. Dec.1689,mar.* of Mousehole. 14 Oct. 1718, ? bur.* 15 Aug. 1776.

Arthur, bap.* 24 Feb. 169?, bur.* 28 Feb. 169?.

AnnHoskin,mar.*=Richard (sen 15 Feb.172?,bur.* | bap.* 17 Feb.1? 29 Oct. 1723. | bur.* 23 Jan. 1

Ann, bap.* 19 Oct.1723 bur.* 14 Nov. 1723.

Pichard of New-=Sarah Berryman of lyn, bap.* 26 May | Paul, bap.* 21 Feb. 1729, mar.* 16 | 173?, bur.* 31 Dec. July 1754, bur.* | 1796, widow, age 77. 17 May 1788, ad- mon. Sept. 23 1788 to widow Sarah.

Ann, bap.* 8 July 1732

Arthur, bap* 26=Elizabeth Beck- Dec. 1737, mar.* | erieg of Paul, 10 May 1760,bur.* | bur.* 29 Sept. 29 Nov. 1764. | 1789.

Arthur of Tiverton 28 Feb. 1757, ba? March, privately, 1795, died 10 Sept. at Tiverton, bur. ? George's Church-y

---

John, bap.* 27 June=Elizabeth, dau. of 1736, mar.* 17 July | John & Elizabeth 1780,will 13 Dec. 1794, | Harvey of Burian, executor only son John. | bap. 21 Feb., 1736, Admon. 2 Feb. 1795. | bur.* 29 Sept. 1789.

Sarah, bap.* 28=George Glasson of Jan. 1760, mar.* | May 1757, bur.* 15 June1780,bur.* | 26 Nov. 1802. 2 Dec. 1802.

Phillis, bap.* 21 Sept.1762,bur.? 23 Nov. 1766.

Ann bap.* 13=Francis August 1761, Russell, mar.* 25 Jan. jun. of 1783. | Paul.

Phillis born* 20 May=..Ayre 1781, bap.* 22 May, | of Wade- mar.* 15 Jan. 1803, | bridge died 2 Sept. 1844.

John, captain in army, bap.* 1 Ap. 1783 died 11 Sept. 1854.

Elizabeth Harvey, born 17=John Rowe, born 6 July 1785, Newlyn, bap.* | Sept. 1767, Trgony, 20 July, mar. 8 May, 1810, | died 21 May 1855, died8July1844,St. Mabyn, | Egloshayle, bur. at bur. St. Austell. | Friends' Cemetery, St. Austell.

William bap.* 24 M 1787, ? died in infan

Anna Maria Hen-=John Jones Pearce, rietta, born? 18 Jan. | born 15 April 1795, 1796, bap. 4 Feb., | Tredenny (Burian) mar. 20 Nov. 1821. | died 10 July 1833, Newlyn. bur.†

Caroline Naomi, born? 28 Nov. 1797, bap. 27 Feb. 1798, died 13 Dec. 1801, bur.at St.James', Piccadilly.

Henry Samuel,=Elizabeth Valentina, born? 2 Sept.1799, | 1st dau. of William bap. 7 Nov.,mar.† | Stoddard, born 8Nov. 11 Dec. 1824. | 1799, at Melcombe Regis.

John Josias Arthur,=C born? 23 June 1801, | R bap. 30 July, mar. | O 4 July 1827, St. Cle- | 1? ments, Truro. | C

Charles William, born? Nov 1833, died § 22 Dec. 1838.

Alice Anne, born 17 Jan.=Rev. Jevon Muschamp 1835, mar. 18 July 1872. | James Perry, born 7 Dec. 1842, at Monmouth.

Helen, born 22 June 1836, died 1 Oct. 1838.

Catherine ? born 13 Jan. mar. 15 Dec. 1?

Henry, born||=Mary, 3rd 5 Oct. 1825, | dau. of James mar.§ 15 Sep. | Thoms, born 1853. | 4 Feb. 1832.

Anna Maria, =William Alfred, born|| born|| 26 Aug. | Alfred 20 July 1829, 1827, died§ 4 | Pearce, mar. 7 May Nov. 1871,mar.§ | first co. 1853 at Fal- 14 June 1853. | bn.13My mouth. | 1826,Greenwich.

Ellen Bradley eld. dau. of William Mil- lett Boase. bn.9 Dec.1827.

Elisabeth, =William Cox born|| 25 July | of Looehee, 1831, mar.§ | born 23 Feb. 22 June 1864. | 1813.

Arthur, born 21 June 183? died§ 8 July 1852.

Henry Samuel, born§ 21 Dec. 1854

Robert Richards, born§ 4 Oct. 1857.

Margaret Elizabeth, born§ 21 Jan. 1861.

Arthur James, born§ 21 Oct. 1863.

Mary Parminter, born§ 21 May, 1866.

John Tregortha, born§ 27 Nov. 18?

THE FAMILY OF BOASE OF PAUL AND MADRON
IN CORNWALL.

THE FAMILY OF BOASE (or Bowes) was settled in the parishes of Paul and Madron at the end of the sixteenth century. Ursula, daughter of William Bowes, was buried at Madron, 14 Dec. 1578 ; Joan, daughter of Edward Bowes, was buried at Paul, 16 Feb. 160⅔ ; and Creston, daughter of Richard Bose, was baptised 27 Feb. 160½, at Paul. The earlier registers at Paul unfortunately perished when the Spaniards burnt the place 23 July 1595. The name was at first usually spelt Bowes, but it is also spelt, like most other names at that time, in a variety of ways; and the spelling Boase became the common one in the eighteenth century. Two entries at Paul about the same person run thus : "Arthur, son of John Boase, bap. 1 Nov. 1652 ;" "Arthur Bowes married Florence, 18 June 1686." The present account is taken from a pedigree entered at the Herald's Office 1810 by Henry Boase, Esq., and duly recorded by Sir Isaac Heard, Garter King at Arms. It reaches from 1681 to 1809, and has been supplemented from family information, from wills, and from the registers. The following notes supply additional particulars taken from these sources. The five marks * † ‖ ‡ § mean throughout "at Paul, Madron, Penzance, London, Dundee" respectively.

SIMON BOWES m. * 8 July 1676 Sara Shutford. He was probably son of the Simon who d. 1697. Administration of his effects was granted at Bodmin, 31 Aug. 1723, to his daughter Sarah, wife of John Bramble, yeoman. The will of his son John is dated at Chioon (in Paul) 9 Oct. 1721, and the probate at Bodmin 1 Oct. 1722. By it he leaves to his sisters Sarah Bramble and Phillis Berryman equal shares of his lease lands, &c. ; to his sister Ursula Boase £20, to be paid to John Boson, gentleman, her trustee, within six years, the executors meanwhile paying him 20 shillings yearly for her : the executors are his brothers-in-law, John Brambel and John Berryman ; his aunt, Blanch Shutford, he leaves to the care of his sisters ; the witnesses are Roger Roberts, Relvisa Maddern, Jane Tonkin. Blanch Shutford may have been Blanch Sampson of Penzance, who married Robert Shutford 1 May 1704, if Robert was brother of Philip Shutford, the father of Sara Shutford, who was mother of John Bowes. The Bosons were then the leading people in the place, and John Boson was probably the well-known Cornish scholar, the correspondent of William Gwavas and others (see Bibliotheca Cornubiensis, under Boson and Gwavas). Juliana, who married John Bowes, * 30 Ap. 1686, was probably the daughter of George Boson, Esq., and this alliance may be the reason of John Boson becoming trustee for one of the family (see Boson pedigree). Another Simon Bowes, probably connected with this one, m. * 3 March 1767. Penelope Ladner of Paul ("with her father's consent," i.e. she was under age : witnesses, Thomas Hoskin, Stephen Barnes).

B

JOHN BOWES, of Tredavo in Paul, who died 1681. There was a family tradition that he came over from Holland and founded the family in Paul. This must be incorrect, but he may have been in Holland, and come back in later life to his native parish. Richard Daniell, one of the chief land-owners in the district, was Governor of Middleburg, under Sir Robert Sidney 1612-14 ; and, through his connections (he married twice there), the Daniell family may have been able to forward the interests of a countryman. This conjecture rests on the fact that in a rent roll (printed further on) of Richard Daniell, in 1657, John Boos appears as holding Tredavo under him at a conventionary rent of £5—the highest rent given. The administration of John Bowes' property was granted at Bodmin, 21 Nov. 1681, to his son Robert, Jane the widow having renounced. Robert probably moved to Penzance, having married Mary Rawling of that place (see below under Boase of Madron and Penzance). It is to be noted that there was probably another John Bowes living at this time in Paul, for an obscure entry in the register seems to read " (Cisley ?) wife of John Bowes, buried 11 April 1661." If so, some of the later children (after Robert and Arthur) here assigned to John Bowes, who died 1681, may be really children of this second John Bowes. At the death of the first John Bowes in 1681, Robert seems to have been the eldest son living. William, perhaps son of this second John Bowes, was baptised * 23 July 1648, ? buried * 28 July 1689, having had a son, William, baptised * 2 April 1678. John, another son (? of the John who died 1681) died 1734, and administration was granted at Bodmin, 17 July 1734, to his son William, and daughter Jane, wife of Thomas John.

RICHARD BOASE of Newlyn, was witness to his brother Arthur's marriage in 1760, and Arthur's daughter, Anne's, marriage in 1763, and died in 1788. Administration was granted at Bodmin 23 September 1788, to his widow Sarah. The witnesses to their marriage in 1754 (by licence) are John Tonkin and Arthur Boase. Both Richard and his widow Sarah Berryman, were buried in Paul Church, and a mortuary paid for them, of 10s. 6d. and a guinea respectively. The will of their son John is dated 13 December 1794. He leaves to his daughter Phillis £500 to be paid her at the age of 21, or on her marriage, if she marry before that age, four per cent. interest being allowed her meanwhile : the same to his daughter Elizabeth Harvey, both sums being charged on his real estates. His only son John is made executor and residuary legatee. The witnesses are Harry and Mary Tonkin and James Pascoe. On 2 February 1795 administration was granted at Bodmin to George Glasson, uncle-in-law and guardian of John Boase, the executor, power being reserved to grant the like administration to John Boase when of age. Stamp £11 10s. John Boase's seal is attached.

It is possible that Richard Boase, who died 1788, had married a first time when very young, for this entry occurs at Paul, " William, son of Richard and Isabella Boase, baptised 6 September 1747, " and the following entry possibly refers to the children of this William. His wife Grace may be Grace, daughter of John and Elizabeth Boase, baptised * 6 December 1747 (same year as her husband).

1789, October 18, baptised Charles and Mary, son and daughter of William and Grace Boase.

The following entries refer to the children of another William Boase living at the same time (unless Richard's son William married Joan, and Grace was the wife of the other William.)

1790, January 25, baptised William son of William and Joan Boase.

1791, July 24, baptised John, son of William and Joan Boase.

1794, April 27, baptised Simon, son of William and Joan Boase.

1797, July 16, baptised Joan, daughter of William and Joan Boase.

1799, July 7, baptised Thomasin, daughter of William and Joan Boase.

1801, March (? April) 12, baptised Charles, son of William and Joan Boase.

1803, April 9, baptised Eliza, daughter of William and Joan Boase.

1805, December 15, baptised Anne, daughter of William and Joan Boase.

1807, September 6, baptised Mary, daughter of William and Joan Boase.

1811, June 9, baptised Richard, son of William and Joan Boase.

John Rowe, who married Elizabeth Harvey Boase in 1810, took out several patents (see Bibliotheca Cornubiensis sub Rawe).

The William, son of John, who married Margaret Martin in 1717, was probably married previously, as there is an entry at Paul, William, son of William Boase, baptised 1 August 1714.

The following entries also occur at Paul :
Marriages—
1632, April 16, William Bawse and Anne.
Baptisms—
1665, October 27, Richard, son of Richard Bowes.
1678, April 2, William, son of William Bowes.
1693, February 25, Mary, daughter of Richard Bowes.
1746, August 3, Elizabeth, daughter of John and Elizabeth Boase.
1747, December 6, Grace, daughter of John and Elizabeth Boase.
1804, October 7 Richard, son of Richard and Jane Boase.
1806, February 22, Elizabeth Lawrence, daughter of Richard and Jane Boase.
1807, May 21, Joannah, daughter of Sampson and Margaret Boase.
1809, March 12, Elizabeth, daughter of Sampson and Elizabeth Boase.
1811, August 4, William Henry, son of Richard and Jane Boase.
1811, October 13, Eliza, daughter of Sampson and Margaret Boase.
Burials -
1689, July 28, William Boase.
1753, July 1, Richard Boase.
1812, July 26, Thomas Boase, age four months, of small pox.
1814, January 23, Elizabeth Boase, age 5 years.

In Burian we find—
William Boase of S. Levan (? moved thither from Paul), married at Burian, 30 May 1737, Alice Taylor of Burian, (? buried 5 April 1784). Their son Charles, baptised 27 December 1737 at Burian, married * 23 April 1766, Elizabeth Uren of Paul, spinster; witnesses, John Gwennap. Philip Madern (? Elizabeth buried 28 January 1794), and had by her Phillis, baptised 11 May 1767, at Burian.

Others occur at Burian -
1782, January 16, buried daughter of William Boase.
1786, August 9, buried Thomasine, wife of William Boase.
1795, January 2, buried John Boase.
1796, February 22, buried William Boase.
1809, December 4, buried Elizabeth Boase, age 25.

At Sennen—
1744, January 6, baptised William, son of William Boase.
1750, June 9, baptised John, son of William Boase.

HENRY BOASE, who died 1827, left behind him an autobiography, from which the following notices of his life have been mainly taken.

Henry Boase, the fourth son of Arthur Boase of Madron, by Jane, daughter of Henry Lugg of S. Keverne, was born at Madron on the third of June 1763, and baptized at the parish church on Midsummer day. As to his family connections he says himself in his autobiography " My paternal grandfather farmed his own little property in the parish of Paul, my maternal grandfather was a Lugg of S. Keverne, where his ancestors were freeholders of old times, and where his family still remain. He purchased some lands both freehold and leasehold in Madron, where he came to reside, and married a Miss Paul, by whom we are related with Luke, Hosking, Wallis, Woodis, and other families. Miss Paul's sister married Hosking of Landithy, and her daughters were married. one to Wallis, another to Thomas Woodis of Alverton. These with the father of Mr. Edmund Paul, surgeon, were first cousins of my mother. Mr. Luke and Dr. Luke are my cousins in the second degree by their mother, a Trevavas; and Mr. Luke's children are doubly related to us, that is by their grandmother, a Trevavas, and by their mother, a Woodis, who was the elder sister of Mrs. John Jones Pearce." He was of weak health, and studious habits, and early gained some knowledge of the classical languages and of French, though the means of instruction within his reach were very small. His father Arthur had been fairly educated, and was a member of the Bowling green and Sporting clubs of the neighbourhood, and was constantly Churchwarden, an office of some note in those days, and which after the squire and the vicar distinguished a chief man in the parish. He was a reader and a politician, and then, what was far from common, had a share of a weekly newspaper, (taken in by several in rotation), the *Sherborne Mercury*, the only paper published at that time in the Western counties. This newspaper was accompanied by a little *Weekly Miscellany*, from which its readers gained small scraps of literary information, and to which Henry Boase afterwards contributed. The Cornish language had not yet wholly died out. ' In my father's early years not a few of the previous generation spoke Cornish, of which he retained many phrases. I remember he used to teach us the Lord's Prayer, sundry proverbs, the numerals &c., in that language."

In 1779 he became a clerk in Mr. Luke's office at Penzance, and gained better opportunities for self instruction than were available at Gear in Gulval, to which his father had removed from Madron in 1774. " Soon after I came to reside at Penzance I had the good fortune to obtain some favour in the sight of a very eccentric man of the name of Hewett, who kept a small, and at that time, the only bookseller's shop in the town. Monthly Magazines were then getting into fashion, about half a dozen of which came to his shop every month, and it was to me a great treat to be permitted to peep between the un-cut leaves, before they were sent home to their owners. With intense anxiety I have often watched the arrival of the monthly wagon, and the removal of my friend's package to his shop, and then passed by the door or made some excuse to go in and see whether it was opened, an operation which the old gentleman, to my great mortification, would sometimes postpone for several days. I reckon it one of the most fortunate circumstances of my life to have fallen into the good graces of the old bookseller, for at that time Penzance afforded very little help towards the acquisition of knowledge,—no book clubs, no public library, no reading rooms, no scientific institutions of any kind; and except a little occasional stir by the novel introduction of Methodism there was nothing to disturb the long established smoking, drinking, and gaming-clubs, of which there were some for all ranks, and for almost all ages. These were distinguished by many ridiculous names, but all agreeing in drunkenness, profanity, and card playing; hard drinking, gaming and swearing, were then considered gentlemanly accomplishments, and destroyed the health and fortune of very many. To the wonderful change which took place soon after the breaking out of the late war, I ascribe much of the increase of population which has since taken place. From the pernicious influence of such society, I was in a great measure preserved by a weak state of health, and a fortunate poverty, which left me very little to spend, and much less than I was anxious to invest in books. This is a sad picture of Penzance, such as it was before I knew it and when I lived there from 1779 to 1784. When I visited it in 1792, I did not observe much difference; but when I again saw it in 1806, I was astonished at the change. Much of the moral change we have seen may be traced to the spread of Methodism, which, while it operated powerfully on the higher orders of society. Smuggling with its concomitant vices of drunkenness and swearing was virtually encouraged by the upper ranks, and was the bane of the miner and the fisherman. Against these especially, Wesley and Whitfield levelled their powerful denunciations, and although their followers were for a long time few and obscure, the evils they condemned were too flagrant to admit of defence. So uncivilized were our miners down to a period so recent as to be within my memory, that one of the terrors of the nursery to quiet froward children was to tell them that the Tinners were rising. When these men felt or fancied some public grievance, they collected in great bodies, and laid the devoted towns and markets under such contributions or restraints as the barbarous multitude thought proper to impose. Among these men Wesley and Whitfield operated a change of incalculable importance not only to the miners but to the community at large."

In 1781, being then clerk to Mr. Luke, he went on business to Falmouth, and as he was very fond of drawing, amused himself with taking sketches of the harbour, and at length wandered within the lines of Pendennis castle, not knowing that it was forbidden ground, it being a time of war, and of great terror about spies; he was consequently arrested and dismissed with a reprimand for the trouble his ignorance had occasioned.

In 1782 he went on horseback to Plymouth on business. Plymouth had hardly yet recovered from the panic occasioned by the combined fleets of France and Spain, which had menaced its destruction three years before, in the month of August 1779. " Of that alarm I have still a vivid recollection, caused probably by the violence of the original impression, when the enemy with apparently an overwhelming force was in sight. Early one beautiful morning the alarm was given that the grand fleet of England, chased by the combined fleets of France and Spain was off the Western Coast. Everybody ran to the hills, from which could be seen at once the British fleet, under Sir Charles

Hardy, 38 ships of the line and a very few frigates, crowding sail to the eastward, and leisurely pursued by the combined fleet, under Count D'Orvilliers, composed of about 70 ships of the line, with a cloud of frigates and smaller vessels. The day was nearly calm, with now and then a little breeze to the northward, so that for the long space of a summer's day the Mount's Bay exhibited the uncommon scene, first, of more than 100 ships of the line assembled, and secondly, of the British Channel fleet flying before the enemy. With the close of the day we lost sight of the fleet off the Lizard, and the second day after, the enemy paraded triumphantly before Plymouth, whence he drew off on the third night, alarmed by a threatening storm with heavy thunder from the south-east. I was told at Plymouth that a single ship might have silenced all the batteries, so wretchedly unprepared were they to sustain any attack."

On the restoration of peace it occurred to him that if he could learn to speak and write French with facility it would be a recommendation, as that was an attainment becoming more necessary in commercial affairs, and far from common among clerks in those days, " So scanty however were my resources at this period, that the expense, though trivial, was a formidable obstacle; but as I could pass over by one of our Mount's Bay boats for nothing, and contemplated only a short stay, it was at length determined that I should go." In the spring of 1784 therefore he landed at Roscoff in Brittany, with the express object of improving his knowledge of modern French, and resided for sometime with a French family at Morlaix, to which he had been introduced by Mr. M'Culloch (father of Dr. M'Culloch, the geologist), a merchant whose acquaintance he had made at Penzance during the war. "Here I was treated very kindly, and passed about nine of the pleasantest months of my whole life. Though Morlaix was a large town, living was then cheap there. My board and lodging were thought liberally paid at the rate of 400 livres, or about £16 a-year. Hairdresser, fencing master, dancing master, and washerwoman, all important personages, and indispensable, were paid 3 livres, or half-a-crown a month each; and an excellent ecclesiastic, L' Abbé Le Roux, gave me instructions in French, in return for my help to a young man, his nephew, whom he wished to learn English. Before the close of the year I found a passage free to Wales in a British vessel, to whose captain I had rendered service as an interpreter at Morlaix, and from Swansea I got a passage home with a captain I had formerly known, so that the whole of this expedition, which was eventually the source of all my success in life, cost less than twenty pounds."

On his return from France, after a brief attempt at setting up in business at Newlyn, he in 1788 went to London, where his knowlege of French proved all-important to him. He became junior corresponding clerk in the bank of Messrs. Ransom, Morland, and Hammersley, in Pall Mall—one of the leading West end firms—and it fell to his lot to conduct much of the correspondence of the emigrants who fled to England during the revolution. To several of these he was able to do much friendly service, and on their return to France, after the peace of Amiens, the Bishop of Troyes and others wrote him very grateful letters.

In 1792 he re-visited Cornwall to see his aged mother, to whom he had for some time sent liberal help. He met his elder brother Arthur (then in the bank at Tiverton, of which he was afterwards a partner), by appointment at Exeter; and they rode on horseback to Penzance, arriving on the evening of the fifth day from his leaving London. It was a tedious journey at that time, in a heavy stage coach, called " The Fly," above forty hours on the road to Exeter, while the only means of travelling further West was on horseback. Of his eighteen days holiday, ten were spent in toilsome travelling.

In 1792 also he became chief clerk, his services having been highly appreciated; and on the first of January 1799 he was admitted as partner in the firm, the business of which had much increased owing to that of Lockhart and Co. being now transferred to it. On Sunday the 26th of October 1794 he had married, at S. Andrew's, Holborn, Anne, the only child of Matthew Craigo, of Walsall, by Anne daughter of John Mason. He had known his future wife for several years. Her father died when she was very young, and she had lived first with her mother's father, and then with her mother who had married secondly Mr. Thing, one of the senior clerks in Ransom's bank. The young couple lived first in Air street, Piccadilly, then from 1795 to 1807 at Knightsbridge, (where eight of their thirteen children were born), and finally at No. 127, Sloane street, Chelsea, which had then an open prospect over what were called "the Chelsea Five Fields," (now Belgrave Square, &c.), and here they remained from 1807 to 1810.

In the terrible winter of 1799-1800, the communication with Hamburgh was stopped for three months, and the wreck of the "Lutine" frigate on the coast of Holland, which was carrying over a great number of merchants and traders, and above half-a-million sterling, brought on a crisis in the business of Northern Germany. The firm of Carpzov of Bremen was one of those which failed, and Mr. Boase went over as soon as the ice broke up, and succeeded in saving part of the amount due to the bank; it was then a common practice on the continent to give up a bankrupt's effects to the home creditors and cheat the foreign ones.

In 1804 he went to Scotland to examine into the affairs of the Dundee New Bank, which was afterwards reconstructed under the proprietorship of Lord Kinnaird and Messrs. Morland, Roase, Baxter and Roberts, and became the parent of the Glasgow Bank: this ultimately led to two of his sons becoming managers of the Dundee Bank; and one of them, Mr. C. W. Boase, has written a very instructive History of Scotch Banking. Mr. Boase had himself written a number of tracts on the famous 'Bullion Question,' which are enumerated in the *Bibliotheca Cornubiensis*.

His health was now so seriously affected by the London winters, that at the close of 1809, he resolved to retire from the business and spend the rest of his life in his native air at Penzance. After a preliminary visit with his wife to make the necessary arrangements, he finally took up his residence there. He resided first in Chapel street, and then on the South Parade; but having purchased about two acres and a half of ground on the west, or Alverton, side of the town for £1000, he built a house there which cost him £3,500 more. It is called Alvern hill, and has a pleasant garden in which the well-known spring, called Alverton well, takes its rise. Not wishing entirely to give up his work, he became a partner in the Bank of Messrs. Batten, Oxnam, and Carne, at Michaelmas 1810, and remained so until Lady Day 1823; soon after which he took over the Penzance Union Bank from Mr. William Boase, and with his two elder sons and Mr. Trevenen James started a new firm on May 1 1823, which was joined by Mr. George Grenfell in 1824. During his residence in London he was well acquainted with Granville Sharp, Robert Owen, and other men, eminent for their philanthropic exertions; was a leading member of the London Missionary Society: and took a considerable part in the foundation of the Bible Society, in conjunction with the Rev. Thomas Charles of Bala, with whom he had become intimately acquainted whilst engaged in distributing, as Mrs. Palmer's banker, her donation of £1000 to the poor beneficed clergymen of Wales. He was also much interested in the formation of schools on the new system of Joseph Lancaster. His correspondence, part of which is preserved in the British Museum (Additional MSS. 29281) gives some interesting details on these matters.

He had originally sympathised with the great French movement of 1789; but, like most Englishmen, recoiled from the atrocities committed by the revolutionists, and

attached himself to the policy of Mr. Pitt. In the years 1803-5 he was senior captain of the Volunteer Corps at Knightsbridge, and spent much time on his duties and on the management of the companies. In the 18 years during which his life was prolonged at Penzance, he returned with fresh zeal to his literary pursuits, corresponded much with Sir Humphrey Davy, and Dr. Edmund Davy, Davies Gilbert, &c., and in 1814 helped Dr. Paris and Mr. Ashhurst Majendie to found the Royal Geological Society of Cornwall; his eldest son Henry afterwards became well known in connection with it by his "Treatise on Primary Geology," and the detailed geological description of every Cornish parish which he contributed to Davies Gilbert's "Parochial History of Cornwall." In 1817-18 he furnished Sir Thomas Bernard with valuable evidence as to the pernicious effect of the Salt laws. He also took an active share in establishing the Public Library at Penzance in 1818, feeling deeply of what value 'such an institution would have been to himself 40 years previously. He was elected a Fellow of the Royal Society of Literature in 1821. He was much esteemed by his fellow townsmen; was elected Alderman, and Mayor in 1816, and took a leading part in Penzance for some years, where he organised a savings' bank, over the interests of which he kept a careful watch. He died 8 April 1827, the long continued east wind of that inclement spring having fatally intensified a chronic disease of the organs of respiration, and was buried in S. Mary's churchyard on the thirteenth of that month. His autobiography, of which much use has been made in this sketch, supplies an excellent instance of the pursuit of knowledge under great difficulties by a poor friendless boy, who won his way in life literally by self help.

His brother Arthur, mentioned in the life, became partner in the Tiverton Bank, 19 April 1808 ; see also Harding's ' Tiverton,' part i, p. 238.

Notices of Henry Boase occur in Davies Gilbert's "Parochial History of Cornwall," C. S. Gilbert's "Historical Survey of Cornwall," and Lake's "Parochial History." The arms of the family are given in C. S. Gilbert, plate 25. They are: Ar. on a chevron engrailed gules 5 bezants between an anchor in base, and 2 birds in chief with wings erect. Or: crest, a demi-lion charged with 3 bezants on the shoulder, and a star on the hip, holding in the fore-paws 5 arrows, 4 in saltire, and 5 in fess on the top. The motto is "Per varios casus."

Of his children, the elder ones born in London were baptised privately by his friend, the Rev. John Townshend, who founded the Deaf and Dumb Asylum in 1792, and died in 1826, and whose memoirs were published in 1828. George was baptised by Mr. Edgcumbe, curate of an Episcopal Chapel in Knightsbridge. The three youngest were baptised at Penzance by the Rev. C. V. Le Grice.

HENRY S. BOASE.

HENRY SAMUEL BOASE, oldest son of Henry Boase, was b. at No. 6 Knightsbridge, London, 2 Sep. 1799, and privately bapt. by the Rev. John Townsend on the 7 Nov. After attending Messrs. Watson's School 32 Sloane street, Chelsea, he proceeded to the Tiverton Grammar School then under the mastership of William Richards LL.D., and in 1815 he was sent to Dublin to study under Edmund Davy, M.D., Professor of Chemistry etc. to the Royal Dublin Society. After some stay in Dublin he gave up his intention of making chemistry his profession, and removing to Edinburgh took up the study of medicine, and going through the usual routine was admitted M.D. in 1821, publishing for his diploma thesis an essay entitled "Dissertatio Medica Inauguralis de Contagio." He now commenced practice as a physician at Penzance, but the profession was so very uncongenial to his taste that he gave it up after a very short trial. He next turned his attention to Geology, and in 1822 was appointed Secretary to the Royal Geological Society of Cornwall in succession to Mr. John Forbes, M.D. (afterwards Sir John Forbes) which place he held until 1829. His first paper in this science was "On the Tin Ore of Botallack and Levant," read at the annual meeting in Oct 1822. During 1829-31 he was employed in ascertaining the nature and boundaries of the Cornish rocks in order that their geographical relation might be accurately delineated in a map. On this work he employed two years and walked 1200 miles, visiting every part of Cornwall and collecting specimens of the rocks, which were deposited in the Geological Museum at Penzance, and form a very valuable series. An account of the journey (with a coloured geological map of Cornwall on the scale of 5 miles to an inch) was published in the Geological Transactions, iv. 166-474. The Geological notices of the Cornish parishes in Davies Gilbert's History of Cornwall as well as in many of the more modern histories are taken from this account. In 1834 he published "A treatise on Primary Geology" a book which still holds its place as a standard work. During some years of the period already spoken of he had been a partner in the Penzance Union Bank, with which establishment he remained connected until its dissolution in Apl 1838. In 1837 he removed to London and took up his residence in Burton Crescent, and on the 4 May of the same year was elected a Fellow of the Royal Society.

In 1838 he left London and went to Dundee when he became managing partner in the firm of Turnbull Brothers, of the Claverhouse Bleachfield; in connection with these works in 1855 he took out a patent for "Improvements in the process of drying organic substances." More recently the Messrs. Turnbull having died and Dr. Boase and his second son having the larger share in the business, the firm has become Messrs. Boase & Co. In Apl. 1870 Dr. Boase came into Dundee to reside, and in 1871 retired from taking any active share in the business. He has published "The Philosophy of Nature 1860" and "An Essay on Human Nature 1865." For an account of his other writings see Bibl. Cornub. i, 29-30. He m. at Madron 11 Decr. 1824 Elizabeth Valentina, eld. dau. of Will. and Mary Stoddard; of his issue of ten children we shall now speak of, (a) Henry, (b) Alfred, (c) Arthur, (d) John, (e) Samuel.

(a) Henry Boase, eld. child of H. S. Boase of Claverhouse, was b. Chapel St. Penzance, 5 Oct 1825, and privately bapt. by the Rev. C. V. Le Grice. At an early age he was adopted by his great uncle Mr. Robert Richards of The Thorns, Alverton, Penzance, with whom he resided many years. He was first educated at the Grammar School, Penzance, under the Rev. George Morris, and afterwards at The High School, Dundee, and then took a situation under Messrs. Turnbull Brothers, at the Claverhouse Bleach Field. There he remained until 1 Jan 1865, when in conjunction with Mr. George Ireland he became the purchaser of the Wellfield Works, Lillybank, where under the firm of Ireland and Boase they became Flax and Jute spinners and manufacturers of hessians, tarpaulings, sacking, etc. On the death of Mr. Ireland on the 4 Dec 1871 H. Boase purchased from his Trustees the other moiety of the business, becoming by this transaction sole proprietor of the works. Mr. Robert Richards dying 11 Nov. 1844, H. Boase became owner of The Thorns, Penzance, subject to the life interest of Miss Richards, and on the decease of that lady, 20 Feb. 1862, he sold that property by auction. He m. 15 Sep. 1853 at Clepington near Dundee, Mary, third dau. of James Thoms by his wife Margaret Jobson, and has issue.

(b) Alfred Boase, second son of H. S. Boase, was born at Penzance 20 July 1829, and privately bapt. by the Rev. W. W. Harvey. After being educated at Penzance and at the High School, Dundee, he in the year 1845 entered the ser-

vice of the Messrs. Richard and Henry Green, shipowners of Blackwall, as a midshipman, and in that capacity made several voyages to the East Indies, Australia and other places. In 1852 the state of his health obliged him to leave the sea, and he entered the Claverhouse Bleach fields (Messrs. Turnbull Brothers) then under his father, as managing Partner, to learn the bleaching business; in course of time he rose to be acting manager, and when in the year 1870 Dr. Boase retired from the direction of the works, Alfred became sole manager with a share in the business, the firm consisting of H. S. Boase and Alfred Boase under the name of "Boase & Co., Yarn millers and calenderers, Claverhouse Bleach field, Trottick mills and St. Andrew's street Dundee." He m. 7 May 1853, at Falmouth, his first cousin, Ellen Bradley, eldest dau. of William Millett Boase, M.D. and has issue.

(c) Arthur Boase, third son of H. S. Boase, was b. Penzance 21 June 1833, and privately bapt. by the Rev. Thos. Vyvyan. He was educated at Glenalmond College, Perthshire, but his health soon commenced failing and he died of consumption at Claverhouse, Dundee, 8 July 1852, and was buried in the church yard at Mains.

(d) John Boase, fourth son of H. S. Boase, was b. Burton Crescent, London, 4 Nov 1837, and bap. St. Paul's Dundee 1838. After being educated at Glenalmond College he entered the establishment of the Messrs. Veitch, Horticulturists, Exeter, to learn ornamental and scientific gardening, but after studying for some years and finding no opening for his labour in England, he sailed for New Zealand where he died of fever at Christ Church 6 Feb. 1865. He m. June 1863 Sarah Jane Knowles and had issue.

(e) Samuel Stoddard Boase, fifth son of H. S. Boase, was b. Claverhouse 19 May 1847. After being educated at Glenalmond College he entered the Lillybank Foundry under his cousins, Pearce Brothers, to learn machine making and mechanical drawing. However in 1870 seeing an opportunity of entering into business he in Dec., in conjunction with Patrick Spence Mudie, son of R. A. Mudie, shipowner, Dundee, took the Bank Mill works, where he now carries on jute spinning, &c., under the firm of Boase and Mudie. He m. at Newcastle-on-Tyne 6 June 1872 Elizabeth, second dau. of James Spence, ship-agent.

———

JOHN J. A. BOASE.

JOHN JOSIAS ARTHUR BOASE, second son of Henry Boase, was b. 23 June 1801 at No. 6 Knightsbridge, London, and privately bapt. by the Rev. John Townshend on 30 July. He was first educated at Messrs. Watsons' School at 32 Sloane street, and afterwards at the Tiverton Grammar School (then under the Mastership of Dr. Richards) from Aug. 1809 to Christmas 1814. He then, after accompanying his younger brother Charles William for a short time to the Grammar School, Helston, was placed in the Bank of Messrs. Batton, Carne and Carne at Penzance where he remained until Midsummer 1817. His father now sent him to France, and during a residence of fifteen months at St. Pol de Leon in Brittany he obtained a good knowledge of the French language. On returning to England in Sep. 1818, he the following Christmas entered the banking-house of Messrs. Ransom and Co London where he staid until May 1824. He then after spending six months on the continent went down to Penzance and took an active part in the recently established Bank of Messrs. Henry Boase, Sons & Co., which consisted of his father Mr. Henry Boase, his brother Mr. H. S. Boase, Mr. Trevenen James and himself, and was called The Penzance Union Bank. However on 30 Dec. 1831 Mr. Trevenen James retired and soon after Mr George Grenfell and his son Mr Pascoe Grenfell joined the firm, which then took the name of

Messrs. Boase, Grenfell, Boase & Co., and J. J. A. Boase and his elder brother became at the same time partners in the Tin smelting firm of Mr. George Grenfell, which then became known as Grenfell and Boase. These two firms were dissolved by mutual consent 21 Apl. 1838, the business of the Penzance Union Bank being sold to the Western District Banking Co., Mr. Boase remaining Manager of the new Company. This arrangement however did not continue many years as in 1844 the business was transferred to Messrs. Ricketts, Enthoven, Turner, Mason, and James, and the old name of the Penzance Union Bank was restored; another rapid change followed, on the 25 Apl. 1846 the firm became Messrs. Ricketts, Fathoven, and James, and in Nov. 1846 the business was dissolved and wound up, and Mr. Boase who had remained Manager throughout the various changes finally retired from business.

Mr. Boase was an Assistant of the Old Corporation of Penzance, which consisted of Aldermen and Assistants, and when the Municipal Act came into operation in 1835 was elected a member of the New Town Council for the West Ward. At the first meeting of the Council he was chosen one of the Aldermen for the same ward. He has been a J. P. of the borough for a very long period, having been appointed in 1836 jointly with Mr. Joseph Carne the first borough magistrates. He was also in 1838 elected a Guardian of the Poor for Penzance.

He succeeded the Rev. C. V. Le Grice as President of the Gentlemen's News Room in January 1859, and held that position until 1864, when it was converted into the Public News Room of which Institution he was then elected President. He was also connected with the Penzance Public Library for many years and was elected President in 1858 in the place of Joseph Carne, Esq. On his resignation of the Presidency in 1874 he was unanimously chosen an Honorary Life Member. Besides the foreign residence before alluded to, Mr. Boase has travelled a great deal, and a portion of his leisure time has been devoted to writing an account of his journeys. This work in MS. occupies twelve volumes folio bound in Russia, and is illustrated by several thousand engravings. For an account of his contributions to various Literary Journals, see Bibl. Cornub. i, 30.

For many years he was employed in numismatic researches, and at one time was the owner of a cabinet consisting of several thousand coins and medals both ancient and modern, but in 1860 he parted with the greater portion of his collection which was sold by Messrs. Sotheby and Wilkinson in London, on the fourth of April and the following days. After the death of Mr. Joseph Carne 12 Oct. 1858, he at the request of Miss Elizabeth Carne, consented to unite with her in carrying on the Penzance Bank jointly with Mr. Philip Marrack and Mr. Thomas Hacker Bodilly, and having an equal share therein; but the partnership was dissolved on the part of Mr. Boase the 30 June 1859.

He m. 4 July 1827 at St. Clement's near Truro, Charlotte second dau. of Robert Sholl by Mary Beard Milford. She was b. Rosewin row, Truro, 30 Oct. 1802, and d. Alverton Vean, Penzance, Wednesday 10 Sep. 1873, bur. the Cemetery 15 Sep. Of his issue we shall now speak of: (a) Charles William, (b) George Clement, (c) Edward Ley, (d) Frederic.

(a) Charles William Boase. eldest child of J. J. A. Boase, was b. Chapel street, Penzance, 6 July 1828 and bapt. by the Rev. W. W. Harvey at St Mary's 19 Sep. He was educated at the Grammar School, Penzance, under the Rev. Geo. Morris, and at the Grammar School, Truro, under the Rev. Dr. Tancock 1841-46. Here he gained Lord Falmouth's medals 1841 and 1842, Dr. Cardew's Exhibition prize 1843, and Lord Falmouth's prize of books in the same year. He next obtained the Elliot Scholarship of the value of £30 per annum, which he held at Exeter College for four years 1846-49. He matriculated at Oxford 4 June 1846, and in the following year gained an open

Scholarship at his College tenable for three years 1847-50. He obtained a second class in the final classical school Trinity term 1850, took his B.A. degree 18 May 1850, and his M.A. 27 Jan. 1863, was elected Cornish Fellow of his College 30 June 1850, Assistant Tutor 1853, Tutor 1855, Lecturer in Hebrew 1859-69, and has been Librarian since 1868. He was ordained 4 Mch. 1855, at Cuddesdon by Bishop S. Wilberforce, but has not proceeded to priest's orders. In 1851 he was proximè accessit for the Arnold Historical Essay on "Carthage," and received a prize of books. He was Master of the Schools 1856, Examiner in Modern History and Law 1857, 1858, 1865, 1866, 1867, 1869, 1870, in Final Classical Examination for honors 1862, 1863, in Modern History 1872 and 1873, for the Pusey and Ellerton Hebrew Scholarship 1861, in the new Combined Examinations for the Pass Schools 1874, 1875. He is known as being one of the joint translators and editors of Ranke's History of England for the Clarendon Press in 1875, and he has contributed numerous articles to The Academy and other literary journals. The account of the Deeds and Writs 1306-1836 in the Dawson Collection in the Penzance Public Library was compiled by C. W. Boase, and is reprinted from The Cornish Telegraph in the Catalogue of the Books of the Penzance Public Library (1874) pp. 336-43.

(b) George Clement Boase, second son of J. J. A. Boase was b. Chapel street, Penzance, 20 Oct 1829, and privately bapt. by the Rev. W. W. Harvey 18 Nov. He was educated at Regent's House Academy and the Grammar School Penzance, and for a short time in 1844 at Bellevue House Academy, Penryn. At the age of 15 in 1844 he entered as a clerk in the Western District Banking Co. Penzance, and continued there when that company was transferred to Messrs. Ricketts, Enthoven, & Co. In 1847 he went to London and engaged himself to Mr. Nehemiah Griffiths, Ship and Insurance Broker, 2 White Hart Court, Lombard street; here he remained for more than three years, and at the end of that period entered the employment of Messrs. Ransom & Co. Bankers, 1 Pall Mall East. On the 29 Apl. 1854 he sailed from Liverpool in the "Great Britain" and landed at Melbourne, Australia, where his first employment was acting as a corrector of the press on "The Age" newspaper; after this he proceeded to the Gold Diggings at Simpson's Ranges, but not meeting with much success and the season proving too dry to admit of gold washing, he was for some time engaged in a general store. On returning to Melbourne he agreed with Thomas Darchy Esq. of Gelam Station, Murrumbidgee River, New South Wales, to become tutor to his family. Accordingly in August 1855 he took up his residence on the Murrumbidgee, and here and on the Lachlan river where Mr. Darchy also owned stations he continued to reside until 1864. During the long period of his residence here his occupation was varied by his acting as paid correspondent of the "Sydney Morning Herald" in the Lower Murrumbidgee and Lower Lachlan districts.

In 1864 he sailed from Melbourne in the "Yorkshire" Capt. Reynell, and landed at Falmouth in a pilot boat on Midsummer eve in the same year. In 1865 he became manager for Messrs. H. M. Whitehead & Co. Australian Provision Merchants, London, with whom he remained until Midsummer 1874, when he retired from business and has since devoted his time to the collection of materials for the second volume of the "Bibliotheca Cornubiensis," the first volume of which in connection with Mr. William Prideaux Courtney he had brought out in Dec. 1873.

(e) Edward Ley Boase third son of J. J. A. Boase was b. Chapel street, Penzance, 26 May 1836, bapt S. Mary's by the Rev. Thomas Vyvyan 22 July, and was educated at Bath under Mr. Shaw, and at Caen in Normandy in 1853. He went to Australia with his brother G. C. Boase in 1854 and was first employed in an office in Hobart Town, Tasmania. After holding various situations for some years both in Victoria and New South Wales, including taking

13

part in the collection of the census of the former colony in 1857, he about 1866 opened a store of his own in Pall Mall, Sandhurst, where he still continues, and has built himself a residence in the vicinity of the town. He m. 1867 Jane Millar and has issue.

(d) Frederic Boase fourth son of J. J. A. Boase was b. at Lariggan, near Penzance, 7 Oct. 1843, and bapt. at S. Mary's 1ˢᵗ Nov. by the Rev. E. Shuttleworth. He was educated at the Penzance Grammar School 1855-57, at Bromsgrove Grammar School, Worcestershire, under the Rev. J. D. Collis, D.D., Aug. 1857, to Dec. 1859 and at Probus under the Rev. Samuel Stead 1860-61. Being articled to Messrs. Rodd and Cornish, Solicitors, Penzance, 24 Dec. 1861, he passed his intermediate examination in London Nov. 1864, and his final examination Jan. 1867, and was admitted an attorney and solicitor 30 Jan. 1867. Since that time he has followed his profession in Exmouth and in London.

CHARLES W. BOASE.

CHARLES WILLIAM BOASE, third son of Henry Boase, was b. No. 6 Knightsbridge, London, 8 June 1804, and privately baptised by the rev. John Townshend, 26 July, removed to Penzance with his father in 1810, and was educated at the Helston Grammar School under Rev. William Stabback. After this he went to France and resided for some time at St. Pol de Leon and obtained a fair knowledge of the French language. On his return he proceeded to Portsmouth where he studied in order to qualify himself for becoming an engineer, but after a time abandoning this intention he with the view of learning Scotch banking entered the Dundee New Bank, in 1821 and after passing through various grades of service, on the retirement of Mr. William Roberts, who went to Glasgow, became manager of the Union Bank, and died 14 Apl. 1832, was appointed manager of the bank. In 1837 he was invited to take the management of the Dundee Bank, and this proposal led to the amalgamation on the 31 Jan. 1838 of the Dundee New Bank with the Dundee Banking Co., established in 1763, Mr. C. W. Boase assuming the management on the 13 March under the title of Cashier. In 1840 the Directors to relieve themselves of some of their duties appointed Mr. C. W. Boase manager; and his brother, Mr. G. C. Boase, became cashier. This position he held till Feb. 1864, when the Dundee Bank was merged in the Royal Bank of Scotland, but he still continued to manage the business till 21 Dec. 1867, when he retired on a pension. On the 10 Jan. 1851 he was presented by the Directors with the sum of two hundred guineas "in consideration of his valuable and efficient services for the past thirteen years." And on the 9 Mch. 1857 he was presented with £300 "in token of their satisfaction at the result of the past year's business." Shortly after he came to Dundee he took a deep interest in promoting the establishment of the Watt Institution, and in 1824 the year when it was called into existence he was elected Secretary and Treasurer which appointments he held until 1828. He arranged the museum of the Institution, occasionally delivered lectures to its members and until its dissolution was one of its warmest supporters.

In 1842 when the town of Dundee became bankrupt, C. W. Boase was one of the trustees elected by the creditors. At one period he was a director of the Public Seminaries, and he also took part in the discussion relative to the improvements of the harbour, his financial knowledge of the business of the town rendering his opinion of considerable value.

In 1850 Mr. Boase became "a believer in the restoration of Apostles to the Church," and one of a small company of like faith worshipping in a room in Whitehall Close under the care of the Rev. G. Crosbie. Soon after he at his own

14

cost erected an elegant little chapel in Bell street to which the congregation removed, and continued there until 30 Nov. 1867 when the present church in Constitution road was opened for service. "Mr. Boase was ordained to the Priesthood in Oct. 1836 and to the Episcopate in Aug. 1851, and after his retirement from business in 1867 had charge of the Evangelistic work throughout Scotland, in consequence of which he removed in Nov. 1870 to Drummond-place, Edinburgh." As a preacher he had a popular style and a happy knack of making himself perfectly understood, so that on occasions when it was announced that he was going to preach many of the outside public attended the church. He originally resided in Meadow Place, Dundee, having a country house at Newport in Fife, but about 1859 went to reside at Balgay House, Dundee. With the intention of providing illustrations of the Scriptures for the members of his own congregation and others, he employed Mr. John Alexander and other artists to make for him copies of many of the most celebrated paintings of the old masters existing in foreign collections; for the proper exhibition of these paintings he built a special gallery at the rear of his house in Meadow Place, and with the hope of encouraging a taste for art in Dundee, these paintings were on more than one occasion lent for public exhibition. One of these pictures, a copy of Leonardo da Vinci's great painting of the Last Supper he presented in 1870 to the Albert Institute, Dundee. the others were removed to Edinburgh, and the collection has now been dispersed.

As an author he has published several works on controversial theology, for which see *Bibl. Cornub.* i. 28, but the publication by which he will be chiefly remembered is entitled "A Century of Banking in Dundee," a mass of facts and figures extending over nearly four hundred pages, and affording most useful information to all persons interested in banking statistics. C. W. Boase died rather suddenly on Friday the 7th June 1872, while staying at Albury, Surrey, "attending a Council of Ministers of the Catholic Apostolic Church;" his remains were interred in the burial ground of the parish church on the 12 June. He m. 9 Dec. 1832 at Dundee Helen, fifth dau. of William and Alison Lindsay, and had issue seven children; of these we propose to speak of two *(a)* Edward *(b)* Clement.

(a) Edward Boase, second son of C. W. Boase, was b. Dundee 16 Dec. 1841, educated at Gothic House, Rottingdean (Mr. Arthur Orlebar's), and at Glenalmond College, Perthshire. He entered the 93rd Sutherland Highlanders in 1860, purchasing his Ensignship 21 Dec. 1860, and his Lieutenancy 10 July 1863. He served in India for some years, and after his return, namely in the commencement of 1868, sold out his commission. Soon after retiring from the army he entered into partnership with Messrs. Robert and Henry Small and his cousin W. L. Boase, under the names of Messrs. Small and Boase. Hemp spinners, twine makers, and manufacturers, having places of business at Rockwell Works. Dundee and Hawkslaw Works, Leven. On the death of Mr. Henry Small in 1869 Mr. Robert Small retired from the firm, and the business was continued by Edward Boase and W. L. Boase under the same title of Small and Boase, until 1 Dec. 1875. At that date they sold the Rockwell Factory and business to W. L Boase. Shortly after, they took a partner, Mr. George Shann; and Edward Boase. W. L. Boase, and George Shann carry on at Leven the business of Hemp Spinners under the name of Small and Boase. He m. 31 Oct. 1871 Emilia only dau. of the late John Bell, solicitor, Dundee.

(b) Clement Boase, third son of C. W. Boase, was b. Dundee 13 May 1846, and educated at Glenalmond College, Perthshire. In May 1864 he entered the Dundee Bank and served as an apprentice until about the end of 1867, when he determined to devote himself to the ministry; accordingly in 1870 he was admitted to the Deaconship in the

C. A. Church, Dundee, but was removed in Jan. 1872 to the Church in Edinburgh, where he still remains. He m. 4 Apl. 1872 Charlotte Hannah, second dau. of Charles D. Young, engineer, Perth.

GEORGE C. BOASE.

GEORGE CLEMENT BOASE, fourth son of Henry Boase, was b. at 127 Sloane street, Chelsea 25 Aug. 1810, and privately bapt. by the Rev. C. Edgecombe; he was educated at the Exeter Grammar School then under the Mastership of Dr. Collins, from thence he proceeded to Queen's College, Cambridge, where he resided 1828-29 but not sufficiently long to take a degree. He then went down to Dundee to visit his elder brother Charles, cashier of the Dundee New Bank, the result of which was that in the summer of 1830 he became a clerk in the Bank, and in August 1832 the directors deeming it desirable to have a confidential clerk to take the cashier's place in his absence, he was offered the appointment and became also a partner in the Bank. As before stated, under C. W. Boase, the Dundee New Bank was amalgamated with the Dundee Banking-Co. in January 1838, and the Dundee Bank Directors wishing to relieve themselves of part of their duties, resolved in April 1840 to make C, W, Boase, manager, G. C. Boase succeeding him as cashier, a position which he held until the amalgamation in February 1864 of the Dundee Bank with the Royal Bank of Scotland, when he became sub-manager, (George Mackenzie, accountant, being made cashier), and so continued until 21 Dec. 1867, when he retired on a pension. Like C. W. Boase, he, in the commencement of 1836, joined the body now generally known as the Catholic Apostolic Church and was ordained to the Priesthood in October of that year. About twelve months after giving up business, that is in the autumn of 1868, he removed to Brighton to take the charge of the Church there. G. C. Boase is the author of several theological tracts, etc., and has been the composer of many fugitive poems. An account of some of his writings will be found in the *Bibl. Cornub.* i. 28. He m. 22 Dec. 1835 at Carolina Port, Dundee, Jane Smyth, fourth dau. of William and Alison Lindsay. Of his issue we propose to speak of *(a)* George William, *(b)* William Lindsay.

(a) George William, eldest son of Geo. Clement Boase, was b. Dundee 6 Feb. 1837, and began his education under the Rev. Alexander Sterling, Tay square, Dundee, subsequently attending for a short time a private school kept by the Rev. T. G. Torry Anderson, in Hawkill place, and afterwards the Dundee Public Seminaries or High School from 1847 to 1850. He went to Gothic House, Rottingdean, (Mr. Arthur Orlebar's) in September 1850, but from bad health had to leave at Midsummer 1851. He then attended the higher classical and mathematical classes at the High School, Dundee, during 1852 and 1853, and on the 12th September in the latter year entered the Dundee Bank as an apprentice, and after passing through the ordinary routine was appointed secretary 14 April 1862, and in February 1864, on the occasion of the amalgamation of the Dundee Bank with the Royal Bank of Scotland became cashier, which position he still holds, (Mr. Mackenzie, cashier, having been promoted to be manager on the retirement of Messrs. C. W. and G. C. Boase in Dec. 1867.) He m. 2 Dec. 1874 at St. Mary Magdalen Church, St. Leonards, Sussex, Florence second dau. of the late Rev. Cuthbert Orlebar of Nottingham, sometime Vicar of Podington, Bedfordshire, by Eleanor, eldest dau. of John Kingston, of the Stamp Office.

(b) William Lindsay Boase, second son of Geo. Clement Boase, was b. Dundee 2 May 1841. He was educated at the High School, Dundee, until 1856, when he went for a year to Luxembourg, and in 1857 to Gothic Hall, Clapham.

In 1858 he entered the office of the late James Bayford, Esq., Proctor. Doctors Commons, and in the same year obtained a clerkship in the Probate Office, where he remained until the spring of 1861. In May 1861 he purchased from Alexander Easson, Esq., a factory at Johnshaven, Kincardineshire, for the manufacture of hemp sacking by hand looms, and subsequently from the same gentleman, the Maxwelltown Factory, Dundee. In 1868 he joined the firm of Boswell and Co., hemp spinners, Leven, and in 1869, when Edward Boase was admitted a partner, the name of the firm was altered to Small and Boase. On 1 Dec. 1875 he purchased from Small and Boase their factory and business at Rockwell Works, Dundee, and carries on these works, and also the factories at Johnshaven and Maxwelltown, in partnership with Mr. Thomas Murdoch who was admitted a partner in 1871, under the firm of W. L. Boase and Co. He m. at St. Andrew's 14 Mch. 1867, Eliza Russell, twin-daughter of Leslie Meldrum, Esq., of Devon Iron Works, and has issue.

JOHN BOASE.

JOHN BOASE the sixth child of Arthur Boase (who d. 1780) was b. Madron 24 Feb. 1771, and bapt. 2 Apl. He was educated and brought up as an architect and a builder, and was the designer and builder of the residences known as Herbier House, Alverne Hill, and a considerable portion of Wellington Terrace, Penzance, etc. Mr. John Boase was a class leader and lay preacher amongst the Wesleyan Methodists until 1835, when he joined the C. A. Church and became the Minister of that denomination at Penzance. He d. Herbier House, Penzance, 23 Mch. 1850 and was bur. St. Mary's churchyard 27 Mch. He m. at Penzance 16 July 1795 Jane, dau. of James Millett, of Helston and had three children, of whom the only survivor

(a) William Millett Boase second son of John Boase was born at Penzance 30 Mch. 1802, and bapt. at St. Mary's chapel 28 July. After being educated at Tiverton Grammar School and at Queen's College, Cambridge, where he kept three terms, he proceeded to Edinburgh in 182— where he studied medicine; on taking his M.D. degree in 1823 he published as his diploma thesis *Disputatio Medica inauguralis quædam de Phrenetide complectens*, Edinburgh, J. Moir, 1823, 8vo. In 1827 Mch. 28, he m. at Madron his first cousin Jane Lydia, 4th dau. of Hen. Boase, and shortly afterwards took up his residence at Falmouth where there was an opening for a physician, owing to the recent death of Richard Edwards, M.D. During 1828-29 he assisted in editing the third and fourth volumes of *The Selector*, or *Cornish Magazine*, a periodical to which he contributed various articles. During 1835 he published a pamphlet entitled *Hints on the exercise of the elective franchise.* This work was in reference to the contested election for Penryn and Falmouth in January 1835, when Jas. Will. Freshfield, (of the firm of Messrs. Freshfields, solicitors to the Bank of England) Robt. Monsey Rolfe, (Solicitor-General, afterwards Lord Chancellor Cranworth), and Lord Tullamore, (afterwards the Earl Charleville), were the candidates, the two former being elected. In the same year he became a member of the C. A. Church, and soon after was appointed a minister of the chapel belonging to that denomination on the Moor Falmouth. In 1857 he left Falmouth and took up his residence at 52, Torrington place, Plymouth, where he still lives. He has for many years past relinquished his professional practice, and is now Minister of the C. A. Church, Plymouth. His only surviving son,

(a) George Clement Boase, second son of Will. Millett Boase, was b. Falmouth 25 Aug. 1838 and bapt. at the C. A. Church by Mr. John Clark 7 Nov. in the same year; after

being educated at the Falmouth Classical School he entered the Royal Marine light infantry, Plymouth division, became Second lieutenant 17 Aug. 1855, First lieutenant 14 Apl. 1859, and Captain 3 Aug. 1867. He m. at St. James's, Piccadilly, London, 22 Oct. 1863 Grace. dau. of James Bone of Budock, and has issue.

BOASE OF MADRON AND PENZANCE.

The following is an account of the various families of the name of Boase in this parish, reconstructed from the Register and other sources ; complete information however is not attainable and some parts of the account are doubtful. All the dates are from the Madron Register, unless otherwise stated.

THE FAMILY OF WILLIAM BOASE.

(A) William Bowes of Penzance had seven children :
(1) Thomas, bap. 12 Feb. 160$\frac{3}{4}$, ? d. infant before 1615.
(2) Gavrigan, bap. 7 Dec. 1606.
(3) Elizabeth, bap. 30 Mch. 1609.
(4) William, of whom presently.
(5) Thomas, bap. 17 Dec. 1615.
(6) Margaret, bap. 22 Sep. 1618.
(7) Blanch, bur. 4 Aug. 1619.

WILLIAM, the third son, bap. 4 Nov. 1610, (Gulval) " son of William Boase of Penzance," ? d. 1662, m. †31 Dec. 1648 Anne, and had by her (who was bur. 12 July 1664, widow,) William and Mary—the latter bap. 21 June 1651.
William the son, ? bur. §13 Jan. 171$\frac{3}{4}$, was probably father of Peter, Elizabeth, William, Arthur, Martin.
(1) Peter, bap. 25 Oct. 1663.
(2) Elizabeth, bap. 27 May 1666.
(3) William, junior, of whom presently.
(4) Arthur of Penzance, bap. 1 Nov. 1676, m. 1st *16 Aug. 1704, Ruth, d. of John Boase of Paul, bap.* 18 Mch. 166$\frac{3}{4}$, bur.* 4 May 1724; he m. 2ndly, †21 Sep. 1724, Margaret Vellenoweth, ' both of Penzance,' ? bur. ‖ 20 Feb. 174$\frac{5}{6}$.
(5) Martin, bap. 24 June 1690, ' son of William Senior.'

WILLIAM, " JUNIOR," of Penzance, bur. 17 July 1716, m. 1675 Cicely, bur. 13 July 1713, ' wife of William Boase, junior of Penzance,' and had by her, William and John.
(1) William of Penzance, bap. 18 Aug. 1678, bur. ‖28 Sep. 1743, had by a first wife, Peter bap 29 Mch. 1703; he m. 2ndly. *25 Nov. 1713, Ursula, d. of Simon Boase of Paul, bap. *20 Ap. 1684, bur. *1 Ap. 1767. and had by her Charles, bap. *3 June 1718, bur. *28 Aug. 1713, John, bap. ‖6 Jan. 172$\frac{1}{2}$, (? do the 2 marriages, given below to John (6), really belong to this John.)
(2) John of Penzance, bap. 26 Dec. 1680, had the following children, Esther, Jacob, Susanna, Honor, Susanna, John.
(1) Esther, bap. 14 May 1700, bur. 23 May 1704.
(2) Jacob, of whom presently.
(3) Susanna, bap. 6 Nov. 1704, bur. 16 Nov. 1708.
(4) Honor. bap. 4 Nov. 1707, bur. 7 June 1708.
(5) Susanna, bap. 19 Sep. 1711, bur. 25 Jan. 171$\frac{1}{2}$.
(6) John bap. 30 Mch. 1713, ? m. 18 Nov. (? Oct.) 1740, Phillis Tregortha, ' both of Penzance,' and had by her,
i William, bap. 29 May 1741.
ii Elizabeth, bap. 4 Jan. 1755.
? Did John m. (2) Mary Parrot in 1749, see below under F.

C

JACOB, bap. 26 Oct. 1702, m. 1st ? 1723, and had Ann, Susanna, Ann, Jacob, Ann; he m. 2ndly. †29 Sep. 1735, Joan Carnpezac of Gulval, and had by her, Helena, William, William.
(1) Ann, bur. ‖ 5 Oct. 1723.
(2) Susanna, bap. ‖ 7 Sep. 1724.
(3) Ann, bap. by Mr. Bower ‖ 27 June 1729, bur. 20 May 1730.
(4) Jacob, of whom presently.
(5) Ann, bap. ‖ 7 Oct. 1733.
(6) Helena, bur.‖ 11 Feb. 174$\frac{4}{5}$.
(7) William, bap. ‖ 15 Dec. 1740, bur. ‖ 21 Dec. 1742.
(8) William, bap. ‖ 27 Sept. 1743.

JACOB, junior, bap. 10 May 1731, ? bur. ‖3 Ap. 1803 mar. † 13 July 1754, Elizabeth Pascoe of Madron, a minor, with consent of guardians, witness Joseph Pascoe, and had by her (who was bur. ? ‖ 12 May 1793; she witn. m. of Elizabeth Pascoe with Henry Williams, † 21 Sep. 1772, the other witness being John Pascoe)—
(1) Elizabeth, bap. 3 Mch. 1755, bur. 5 Mch. 1756.
(2) Elizabeth, bap. 5 Feb. 1756, m. † 2 Jan. 1781, Francis Mathews, both of Penzance.
(3) Thomas, bap. 16 Ap. 1759.
(4) Hannah, bap. 16 Mch. 1761.
(5) Susanna, bap. 24 Jan. 1763, ? m. † 2 Oct. 1790, Thomas Oliver, ' both of Penzance.'
(6) Mary, bap. 8 Mch. 1765.

THE FAMILY OF REYNAULD BOASE.

(B) Reynauld Boase, bur. 14 Jan. 164$\frac{3}{4}$, m. 1st † 1 Feb. 162$\frac{1}{2}$ Mary, bur. 21 Nov. 1639, by whom he had Mary bur. 26 Dec. 1647, and Richard bur. † 25 Nov. 1639 : he m. 2ndly Eleanor, bur. 16 Aug. 1646, and had by her Dina, bap. 4 Aug. and bur. 12 Aug. 1646.

THE FAMILY OF ROBERT BOASE.

(C) Robert Boase, bur. ‖ 26 Feb. 174$\frac{4}{5}$, m. † 12 Aug. 1716 Margaret John, ' both of Penzance' (? his second wife, see Pedigree sheet) : their children were
(1) Robert bap. ‖ 20 May 1720, m. † 29 June 1747 Eleanor Bisky, ' both of Penzance.'
(2) James, bap. 18 Ap. 1724, bur. ‖ 10 July 1724.
(3) James, bap. 29 Nov. 1726.
(4) John, bap. 1 Mch. 172$\frac{7}{8}$.
(5) William. bap. 2 Feb. 173?.
(1) Constance, bap. ‖ 12 Dec. 1716, m. † 13 July 1746 John George, ' both of Penzance.'
(2) Ann, bap. ‖ 25 Mch. 1718, m. † 29 Sep. 1744 Richard Batten, ' both of Penzance.'
(3) Elizabeth, bap. ‖ 14 Mch. 172$\frac{1}{2}$.
(4) Margaret, bap. ‖ 18 Ap. 1733 ? bur. ‖ 10 Dec. 1811, ' spinster,' age 76.'
(5) Mary, bap. ‖ 23 Ap. 1735, bur. 14 June 1738.
(6) Jane, bap. ‖ 23 Ap. and bap. ‖ 4 Aug. 1738.
A Robert Boase of Penzance administered at Bodmin 22 Nov. 1740 to his father Robert, mariner.

THE FAMILY OF TONKEN BOASE.

(D) Tonken Boase, bur. 6 Dec. 1703, fellmonger, ' assistant ' in Corporation 1693, m. † 1654, and had—
(1) Jacob of Penzance, bap. 2 June 1666, bur. 26 Ap. 1702.

(2) Tonken. jun. of Penzance, bur. † 23 Feb. 170⅜, m. ?
1699, and had Rachel, bap. 16 July, and bur. 31 Aug. 1700
(1) Joan, bur. 1 Mch. 165¼.
(2) Ann, bap. 20 Oct. 1661.

The Family of Sampson Boase.

(E) Sampson Boase, bur. ‖ 15 July 1778, m. † 5 Nov.
1725 Margaret Perleggan, ' both of Penzance,' and had by
her (? bur. 20 Feb. 174⅜, or 10 Dec. 1747).
(1) Sampson, bur. ‖ 23 Nov. 1729.
(2) Sampson, bap. ‖ 1 Nov. 1730.
(1) Jane bap. ‖ 15 Jan 172⅔, ? d. infant before 1734.
(2) Ann, bap. ‖ 30 Sep. 1727, bur. ‖ 11 Mch. 172⅞.
(3) Jane, bap. ‖ 4 Feb. 173⅜, m. † 28 Aug. 1757 John
Smith of Fourth Regiment, witn. Sampson Boase and John
Sampson.
(4) Margaret, bap. ‖ 22 Mch. and bur. ‖ 24 Mch. 173⅞.

The Family of John Boase.

(F) John Boase, victualler, Penzance, d. 1775 ; administration at Bodmin 12 July 1775 to his widow Mary : m.
by licence † 6 Nov. 1749 Mary Parrot of Penzance (? aunt
of Josiah Parrot senior, and witn. to his marriage with Ann
Sampson † 27 Jan. 1768) ; she was bur. ‖ 21 Dec. 1779 ; and
her will, made 30 June 1778 as a widow (witnesses William
Ustick, William Stone) was proved at Bodmin 12 May
1780 ; in it she mentions her sons William and Joseph, but
leaves her property (which perhaps came from the Parrot
family) to Josiah, son of Josiah Parrot of Penzance, and
John son of John Mitchell of Penzance : administration was
granted to her son William, as guardian of Josiah Parrot
jun., and to John Mitchell the father. Her children were—
(1) Mary, bap. 29 July 1750, ? dead before 1778, m. +
11 Oct 1772 John Michell, ' both of Penzance,' by licence,
witn. Alice Michell, Ann Tonkin.
(2) William, b. ? 1755, ? m. † 16 May 1777 Alice Michell,
(see below *G*).
(3) Joseph, bap. ‖ 7 June 1756, d. before 1788, m. † 18
June 1781 Honor Thomas, ' both of Penzance,' and had by
her (who m. 2ndly † 30 July 1788 Henry Polglase) a son
John bap. 2 Oct. 1782.

The Family of William Boase.

(G) William Boase, surgeon at Redruth, (see above *F*,
whose father perhaps also moved to Redruth previously, b.
circa 1753, d. 30 Jan. 1813 Redruth, m. † 16 May 1777 Alice
Michell, ' both of Penzance ' : their children were William,
Matthias John, Jane Ann, Sarah, Esther, Alice.
(1) William, b. ? 1786, of whom presently.
(2) Matthias John, surgeon, Redruth, b. 1793 Redruth, d.
30 Mch. 1858 Redruth, bur. 5 Ap. his will proved at Bodmin 6 July 1858, effects under £3000, executors John Bennet and William Davey Boase of Pentroa villa, Avenue
road, Regent's park, London.
(1) Jane Ann, b. 1778.
(2) Sarah.
(3) Esther.
(4) Alice.

William, b. ? 1786 Redruth, d. 1843 Liskeard, aged
57 ; educated for the medical profession, but became a
printer at Liskeard 1805, Mayor 1836, m. Margaret Davey
of Redruth, and had by her William Davey Katherine,
Mary, Ann Bennett.

(1) William Davey, solicitor, and Mayor of Liskeard
1841, 1849, 1852, one of the Inspectors appointed by the
Charity Commissioners for England and Wales, b. 28 Sep.
1818 Liskeard, bap. 28 Sept. 1821 Liskeard church, d. 174
Adelaide road. Hampstead, 25 Mch. 1866, bur. 29 Mch. at
Kensal Green, will proved 8 May 1866 by widow Martha.
He m. 1851 Martha Fookes of Liskeard. and had by her—
1 William Francis Fookes, b. 11 Nov. 1852.
2 Arthur Godolphin, b. 1834, d. inf.
3 Edward, b. 1 Ap. 1858.
4 Richard Davey, b. 26 Oct. 1859.
5 John Atholstan, b. 1862, d. inf.
6 Charles, b. 15 Mch. 1864, d. 19 Dec. 1873 Plymouth.
1 Margaret, b. 6 June 1855.
2 Mary, b. 1856, d. inf.
3 Katherine, b. 13 Oct. 1861.
(1) Katherine. b. 13 Dec. 1807. d. 6 Sep. 1823.
(2) Mary, b. 3 May 1810, d. 27 Ap. 1828.
(3) Ann Bennett, b. 7 Dec. 1814, d. 12 Jan. 1836.
(Blanch Michell Boase of Redruth, spinster, d. 30 Jan.
1870 Redruth : will proved 16 Feb., effects under £1500.)

The Family of John Boase.

(H) John Boase of Penzance, m. † 27 Oct. 1717, Grace
Stephens of Penzance. ? bur. ‖ 6 Nov. 1739, or did he m.
2ndly Jane Carter of Penzance, † 27 Mch. 1722. His issue
were Elizabeth, John. Roger, John, Henry and Francis.
(1) Elizabeth, bap. ‖ 5 June and bur. ‖ 8 June 1718.
(2) John, bap. ‖ 30 May 1721, ? d. inf. before 1724.
(3) Roger, bap. ‖ 14 June 172⅜.
(4) John, bap. ‖ 26 July 1724, m. † 29 Oct. 1748 Alice
Wallish of Penzance, and had by her—
1 Mary, bap. ‖ 26 Dec. 1749.
2 John, bap. ‖ 27 Dec. 1751, ? bur. ‖ 27 July 1794,
m. † 25 Jan. 1773 Dorothy Sampson of Madron, (witn.
Sarah Trexise, Ann Scaddan), and had by her, Jane, bap. ‖
21 Nov. 1773.
4 Henry, bap. ‖ 11 Nov. 1755.
5 Francis, bap. ‖ 27 Mch. 1758, m. † 29 Oct. 1781,Mary
Kitto, (both of Penzance, witn. John Boase, Ann Sampson),
bur. 14 Jan. 1785 : ? he m. 2ndly † 19 Ap. 1800 Elizabeth
Shephard (both of Penzance, witn. Thomas Shephard): by
his first wife he had—
i Francis, bap. 7 Oct. 1782, bur. ‖ 3 July 1785.
ii Mary, bap. ‖ 27 Sep. 1784.
6 Honor, bap. ‖ 24 Feb. 1760.
(5) Henry, bap. ‖ 21 Feb. 172⅜, d. ‖ 19 Jan. 1780, administration 13 Mch. 1780 to creditors, the widow Jane having
renounced: he m. † 22 Jan. 1759 Jane Tredennick of
Camborne, witn. George Connock, Francis Boase : their
children were—
1 Hannibal, bap. ‖ 9 Mch. 1760, bur. ‖ 26 Dec. 1762.
2 Jane, bap. 28 Feb. 1762, bur. ‖ 26 Dec. 1762,
infant.
3 Hannibal Johns, bap. 16 Sep. 1765, m. Esther, and
had by her—
(i) Hester, bap. ‖ 8 Dec. 1793.
(ii) Mary, bap. ‖ 13 Sep. (or 11 Sep.) 1795.
(iii) English Fox, bap. ‖ 24 Jan. 1802.
(iv) Jane, bap. ‖ 11 Sep. 1804, privately.
(v) Sarah, bap. ‖ 28 Sep. 1806, bur. ‖ 7 Dec. 1812.
(vi) Elizabeth, bap. ‖ 9 Nov. (or Dec.) 1812.
4 Henry, bap. ‖ 23 Oct. 1767.
5 Thomas, bur. 4 Oct. 1772.
6 Thomas, bap. ‖ 19 June 1780. bur. ‖ 17 Apl. (or Mch.)
1819, ' married'; by his wife Ann he had—
(i) Thomas, bap. ‖ 22 Ap. 1804.

(ii) Henry Hocken, bapt. ‖ 1 Dec. 1806, ? bur. ‖ 6 Mch. 1811, inf.
(iii) Francis, bap. ‖ 9 Sep. 1810, bur. 22 Jan. 1812, inf.
7 Jane, (? twin with Thomas), bap. ‖ 19 June 1780.

(6) Francis, bap. ‖ 6 Jan. 172$\frac{5}{6}$, bur. ‖ 10 Feb. 1799; will 17 Jan. 1797, witn. William Thomas, Hester Boase, Hannibal Johns Boase, proved 9 Ap. 1799: he m. † 21 Apl. (or 27 Apl.) 1767 Grace Dennis, 'both of Penzance,' (witn. Catherine and Mary Dennis), bur. ‖ 24 Oct. 1779, and had by her Francis, John, Peter Dennis, Grace Dennis, Mary, Catherine—all of whom are named in the will.

1 Francis. b. 27 Mch. 1769.
2 John of Castlehorneck, b. 19 Dec. 1771, bap. ‖ 24 Feb. 1772, d. 24 Mch. 1836, m. at Stonehouse (m. by Rev. Dr. Bidlake) 13 Aug. 1810 Susanna 3rd d. of Thomas Field of Stonehouse, and had by her—
i John b. 19 June 1817, d. Nov. 1852.
ii Francis b. 8 Feb. 1819. Educated at University college, M.R.C.S England, 1841, L.S.A. 1842: District Medical Officer of the Penzance Union, Mayor of Penzance 1868 and 1871, Captain of the First Duke of Cornwall Rifles. Resides at Buriton house, Alverton, Penzance: m. Paul, 19 May 1852 Margaret second dau. of Philip Marrack, banker, Penzance.
i Susan Elizabeth Field b. 26 Feb. 1812, and bapt. ‖ 26 May, m. 1836 Frederick John Gruzelier, now (Mch. 1876) retired staff commander R.N.
ii Mary b. 14 Feb, 1814, and bapt. 7 Mch. d. 14 Feb. 1830.
iii Emily b. 23 Oct. 1815, d. Sep. 1833.
3 Peter Dennis, b. 22 Feb. 1775 bap. 10 June 1776.
1 Grace Dennis, b. 27 Mch. 1770, bap. ‖ 3 Dec. 1770, m. † 18 Nov. 1795 Thomas Broad jun. of Penzance, by licence, witn. Francis Boase, Thomas Broad.
2 Mary, b. 9 Apl. 1773, bap. ‖ 28 June 1773.
3 Catherine b. 22 July 1776, m. (? 1802) Thomas Field of Stonehouse and Marazion, and had by him Hannah, b. 1803, bap. 1808; Mary Boase, b. 14 Jan. 1804, bap. 12 Aug. 1808; Eliza, b. 1805, bap. 1808; Jane, b. 1807, bap. 1808.

The Family of Peter Boase.

(I) Peter Bowes, or Boas, *alias* Gymbale, bur. † 16 Aug. 1601, m. † 10 Nov. 1583, Elizabeth Tonken, ? bur. 12 † Jan. 163$\frac{3}{4}$, 'widow,' and had by her Thomas, bap. 18 Oct. 1592, bur. † 16 Jan. 159$\frac{2}{3}$; and Elizabeth, bap. † 8 June 1600, ? bur. 22 May 1677.

Jane, dau. of (another) Peter Boase was bap. 19 Mch. 164$\frac{2}{3}$, bur. 18 July 1714 'of Penzance, spinster.'

Roger Gymbal, m. † 24 July 1625, Joan. A Roger Bowes was bur. † 12 May 1634, perhaps the same person.

Did the name *Tonken* come into the family from the marriage of Peter Bowes with Elizabeth Tonken?

The Family of William Boase.

(J) William Boase of Madron, married and had issue—
(1) Richard, bap † 2 Feb. 172$\frac{2}{3}$
(2) Susanna, bap. † 12 May 1725, m. † 26 Feb. 1759, John Vinicombe, 'both of Madron,' witness John Tonkin (Arthur Boase witnessed m. of William Vinicombe with Elizabeth Hosking, 'both of Madron,' † 18 May 1761, the other witness was Richard Trembath.)
(3) Margaret, bap. 18 June 1727.

The Family of John Boase.

(K) John Boase of Madron, m. † 31 July 1768, Elizabeth Lawrence of Madron, and had by her—

(1) William of Madron, bap. † 10 Nov. 1771, m. * 21 May 1796, Martha, d. of Richard and Blanch Caddy of Paul (witn. John Boase, Richard Caddy), bap. * 19 Aug. 1770, bur. † 9 Nov. 1804, and had by her—

1. Alice, bap. † 6 July 1794.
2. Elizabeth, bap. † 13 Mch. 1797, privately.
3. Martha Caddy, bap. † 10 Feb. 1799.
4. Isabella, bap. † 5 May 1801, privately.
5. John, bap. † 26 Aug. 1802, privately.

(2) Richard, bap. 5 Ap. 1774.
(3) Elizabeth, bap. † 7 Mch. 1779, bur. † 28 Jan. 1781.
(4) Elizabeth, bap. † 12 Ap. 1784.

The Family of William Boase.

(L) William Boase of Penzance, m. † 15 Dec. 1798, Mary Wesley of Penzance, and had by her—
(1) William, bap. ‖ 31 Mch. 1799, d. ‖ 30 Nov., and bur. 3 Dec. 1807, age 9.
(2) Mary, bap. 7 Sep. 1800
(3) Nancy, bap. 14 Nov. 1802.
(4) Betsy, bap. 6 Feb. 1805.
(5) Joseph, bap. 27 Aug. 1809.
(6) Margaret, bap. 4 Aug. 1811, 'd. of William and Mary,' bur. ‖ 26 July 1812, 'infant.'

The following entries also occur at Madron: a few, already given, are repeated for the sake of comparison:

Marriages—

1597, Oct. 28, Richard Bowes, m. Florence.

1709, Dec. 26, Thomas John of Penzance m. Jane Boase of Gulval.

1722, March 27, John Boase m. Joan Carter, both of Penzance.

1728, Dec. 24, William Richards m. Mary Boase by license, both of Penzance.

1745, Jan (? June) 3, John Boase m. Elizabeth Martin, both of Penzance, (see bapt. Paul 1746, col. 3.)

1751, May 27, John Boase m. Florence Guy, both of Penzance, (? Florence bur. ‖ 15 Jan. 1765.)

1760, July 7, John Kirkby m. Grace Boase, both of Penzance.

1767, June 8, John Boase, widower, m. Elizabeth Berriffield, both of Penzance, witnesses Thomas Webb, Peter Boase.

1770, Feb. 17, John Boase m. Mary Osborne, both of Penzance, witnesses Elizabeth and Phillis Sampson.

1770, June 25, John Boase, carrier. m. Mary Hoskin, both of Penzance, witnesses Mary Barel (?), William Tremenheere junior.

1772, July 11, James Ladner m. Mary Boase, both of Madron, witnesses John Ladner, Richard Batten.

1783, Jan. 4, Charles George, a soldier in the Cornish Militia, m. Elizabeth Boase, both of Penzance.

1784, Jan. 26, William Boase m. Susanna Sampson, both of Penzance, witness Thomas Sampson.

1785, April 11, William Harden of Amsworth in Hampshire, mariner, m. Sarah Boase of Penzance, witnesses William Boase and Susanna Sampson Boase.

1789, May 11, Henry Luke m. Jane Boase, both of Penzance.

Baptisms—
1592, Oct. 18, Thomas son of Peter Bowes.
1638, Oct. 21, Joseph son of Richard Bose.
1727, May 13, Joseph son of John Bonse at Penzance.
1729, May 25, Grace, dau. of John Boase at Penzance.
1731, Oct. 16, Grace dau. of John Boase at Penzance.
1731, Nov. 29, Susanna dau. of John Boase at Penzance.
1734, June 2, Anne dau. of John Boase at Penzance.
17⁴⁴₂, Feb. 12, John and Elizabeth, son and dau. of John Boase at Madron.
1752, March 27, John son of John Boase at Madron, privately.
1752, April 6, Margaret dau. of John Boase at Penzance.
1753, Sept. 9 (? 29), Margaret dau. of John Boase at Madron.
1758, 4 Sep. (? Aug.) Catherine dau. of John Boase at Penzance.
1763, Oct. 9, Jacob son of John Boase.
1771, Ap. 24, William son of John Boase at Penzance.
1771, Sep. 28, Alice dau. of John Boase at Penzance.
1772, Dec. 4. Anne dau. of John Boase at Penzance.
1775, Sep. 5, James and Robert sons of John Boase at Penzance.
1776, Sep. 21, James son of John Boase at Penzance.
1777, July 30, son of John Boase at Penzance.
1786, Dec. 4, Francis son of Francis Boase at Penzance.
Burials—
1578, Dec. 14, Ursula dau. of William Bowes.
159¼, Jan. 30, Agnes wife of Edward Bose.
1632, Dec. 4, Margaret wife of Ralph Bons.
163¾, Jan. 12, Elizabeth Bons widow
1634, May 12, Roger Bowes.
1639, Feb. 22, Ralph Bowes.
1637, Ap. 21, John Boas.
1666, May 31, Katherine Bose.
1677, May 22, Elizabeth Boase.
1704, Dec. 17, Ann Boase widow, of Penzance.
170⁴₉, Jan. 5, Joan Boase widow, of Penzance.
1714, July 18, Jane Boase, spinster, of Penzance.
1717, Jan. 13, William Boase at Penzance.
1718, June 5, Hannah Boase at Penzance.
1724, June 6, John Boase at Penzance.
1729, Aug. 22, Elizabeth Boase at Penzance.
1730, May 13, Grace dau. of John Boase at Penzance.
1732, Oct. 7, Susanna dau. of John Boase at Penzance.
1755, May 22, Hannah Boase at Penzance.
1739, Nov. 6, Grace Boase at Penzance.
1742, June 13, Anne Boase at Penzance.
1743, April 19, John Boase at Penzance.
1743, Sept. 28, William Boase at Penzance.
174¾, Feb. 26, Robert Boase at Penzance.
174⁴, Feb. 27, John Boase at Penzance.
1745, June 24, Anne Boase at Penzance.
174⅚, Feb. 20, Margaret Boase at Penzance.
1747, Dec. 10, Margaret Boase at Penzance.
1749, May 5, John Boase at Penzance.
1767, June 12, Robert Boase, infant.
1769, Oct. 6, Elizabeth Boase.
1770, March 28, John Boase.
1774, Aug. 2, Margaret Boase.
1779, July 15, Robert son of John Boase at Penzance.
1785, Jan. 14, Mary Boase at Penzance.
1786, April 26, Alice Boase at Penzance.
1787, Jan. 2, Margaret Boase at Madron, age 72.
1787, April 8, Henry Boase at Madron.
1793, May 12, Elizabeth Boase at Penzance.
1794, July 27, John Boase at Madron.
1796, Sept. 21, John Boase at Madron.
1799, Ap. 5, Joan Boase at Penzance.
1805, March 24, William Boase from Gulval.
1806, July 11, John Boase at Penzance.

1810, April (? March) 17, Thomas Boase at Penzance 'married.'
1811, Dec. 10, Margaret Boase, spinster, at Penzance, age 76.

BOASE OF GULVAL, LUDGVAN, CAMBORNE AND FALMOUTH.

GULVAL—
Marriages—
1699, June 29, Rawlen Boas ('Gullicus') m. Janetta Nichols.
("1709, Dec. 26, Jane Doase of Gulval, m. Thomas John of Penzance," Madron register).
1738, May 27, John Boase of Camborne m. Lucretia French of Gulval.
Baptisms—
1610, Nov. 4, William, son of William Boase of Penzance.
1700, Oct. 6, Sampson, son of Rawlen Boase, (born 1 Oct.)
1736, Aug. 29, Ester, dau. of Jacob Boase.
1798, July 1, Jane, dau. of Richard and Margaret Boase.
1799, Oct. 2, Richard, son of Richard and Margaret Boase (bur. 6 Oct),
1804, Oct. 26, Richard, son of Richard and Margaret Boase.
Burial—
("1805, March 24, William Boase of Gulval," Madron register.)
CAMBORNE—
Baptisms—
1736, July 24, William son of Robert Boase.
1742, July 18, Robert son of Robert Boase.
1742, Nov. 15, Susanna dau. of John Boase.
William Boase of Camborne had a son Robert, bap. Ludgvan, 28 Jan. 173¾; bur. Ludgvan, 15 June 1783, who m. Anne Giles 7 May 1758, Ludgvan, 'both of Ludgvan,' and had by her, (1) Edward, bap. 29 July 1760. Ludgvan, died 17 March 1761, (2) Robert, bap. 24 May 1768, Ludgvan.
LUDGVAN -
Marriage—
1780, May 8, William Boase m. Joan Michell, 'both of Ludgvan.'
Baptisms—
173⁴₉, Jan. 14, John son of John Boase privately, bur. same day.
17¾₂, March 9, Christian dau. of John Boase.
Burials—
1761, March 17, Edward Boase.
1860, Jan. 3, died Robert Boase of Ludgvan, formerly of Zennor; he m. Wilmot: his will was proved at Bodmin 26 Oct. 1860: he had a brother Christopher.
FALMOUTH—
Baptisms—
1827, March 4, William son of William and Catherine Boase.
1829, Jan. 11, Anne Hocking, dau. of William and Catherine Boase.
Burial—
166¼, Jan. 29, Jane wife of Thomas Boase.

SOME ACCOUNT OF FAMILIES WHICH HAVE INTERMARRIED WITH BOASE OF PAUL, MADRON, ETC.

BEARD OF PAUL AND PENZANCE.
JOSEPH BEARD, Tin merchant, is believed to have been bur. ‖ 14 Nov. 1745, and to have m. a cousin called Mary

(? dau. of a clergyman) in 1724. Their twelve children were (1) John, (2) Joseph, (1) Hannah, (2) Susanna, (3) Catherine, (4) Catherine, (5) Sarah, (6) Sarah, (7) Charlotte, (8) Mary, (9) Lydia, (10) Lydia. (A Mrs. Mary Beard was bur. ‖ 4 June 1785, widow.)

(1) John of Halwin in Paul after his wife's death removed to Penzance, where he resided in a house in Parade street, which is now used as offices by Messrs. Rodd and Cornish, solicitors. He was mayor of the town 1776, 1784, 1794, and 1799, d. Kenegie, Gulval, 14 Feb. 1805, in his 63rd year. He m. Madron 28 July 1766 Elizabeth dau. of Richard Pearce of Kerris, in Paul (when the witnesses were Jane Pearce and Caroline Borlase). She d. Exeter 18 Nov. 1778, aged 37, monu. Madron. Their children were i. John, ii. Mary, iii. Elizabeth, iv. Hannah.

i John, Attorney, Town Clerk of Penzance, 1794-1828, published in 1825 James 1st's Charter to Penzance. Bapt. 16 Apl. 1769, d. Penzance 6 Nov. 1828, m. † 10 Feb. 1800 Lucy dau. of Mr. Bromley of Penzance, she d. Penzance 27 Nov. 1829, aged 52. Their children were 1 John Ley privately bapt. 4 Dec. 1806, who is believed to have d. 1865; 2 Joseph in Australia; 3 James; 1 Emma d. 185—, before her husband, m. James Gwavas Beckerleg, solicitor, Penzance, and Clerk of the Stannaries; 2 Eliza living at Falmouth; 3 Another daughter living at Falmouth.

ii Mary d. Southmolton, Devon, 21 Sept. 1812, aged 41, m. * 30 Mar. 1793 Rev. William Harris (Arundell) of Kenegie, Gulval (witnesses Elizabeth and Hannah Beard), he d ‖ 19 Feb. 1798, aged 38.

iii Elizabeth bapt. 24 Feb. 1769, m. Rev. Thomas Amory now Vicar of St. Teath.

iv Hannah living 1814.

(2) Joseph b. 1744, subscribed to Carew's Cornwall 1769, d. 8 Mch. 1790, aged 46, bur. * 12 Mch. 1790.

(1) Hannah bapt. † 20 Jan. 172$\frac{4}{5}$.

(2) Susanna bapt. † 18 July 1726, m. † 28 Jan. 1758 Jacob Daniell of Truro (witnesses Mary Cole, Mary Beard).

(3) Catherine d. an infant.

(4) Catherine b. 1728, d. 9 (11) Jan. 1778 or 1779, aged 50, m. † 17 Aug. 1753 George Ley of Penzance. *See* Ley.

(5) Sarah d. an infant.

(6) Sarah bur. ‖ 20 Nov. 1738.

(7) Charlotte bur. 14 Feb. 1810, aged 76, m. † 1 Sep. (? 25 Aug.) 1763 Jonah Milford of Truro (witnesses John Painter, Joseph Beard), m. by Rev. James Parkin, lecturer of Penzance. *See* Milford.

(8) Mary ? bur. 6 July 1762.

(9) Lydia d. an infant.

(10) Lydia d. in an asylum.

There were also other families of the same name, *e.g.*:

(1) Ralph, who had a seat in Penzance Church 1674. He was in business and issued a token 1667. He is thought to have m. 1664 Dorothy, bur. ‖ 15 Dec. 1728. The children were—

i Ralph bapt. † 12 Oct. 1665.

ii Samuel bur. † 3 Oct. 1675.

i Priscilla or Prudence bapt. 24 Mch. 166$\frac{5}{6}$.

ii Joan bapt. 30 Mch. 1667.

iii Elizabeth bapt. † 20 June 1669, and is thought to have m. † 16 Aug. 1719 Richard Greby.

(2) Richard of Penzance, who m. Burian, 5 Nov. 1697, Mary (Harvey ?) of Penzance, and had by her—

i Joseph d. 11 Nov. 1745 or 46, bur. Penzance, 14 Nov., aged 48. Unm.

ii Harry, bapt. 15 Apl. 1702.

iii Samuel, bapt. 23 Jan. 170$\frac{3}{4}$.

i Mary, bapt. 3 Dec. 1700, ? m. † 31 July 1739. Peter Carveth "both of Madron."

(3) Deborah of Penzance, d. 15 Oct. 1816 aged 79, m. Madron, 21 May, 1771, Rev. Anthony Williams, V. of St. Kevern (witnesses, Susannah Beard, Hannah Pascoe), he d. 2 Sep. 1816, aged 78.

(4) Grace, m. † 2 Sep. 1732, John Pascoe, junr., "both of Penzance."

(5) Mrs. Lydia, bur. ‖ 28 May 1787.

(6) Mrs. Susanna, bur. ‖ 21 Sep. 1810.

(7) Jacob son of Jacob, bap. * 1 Feb. 172$\frac{3}{4}$.

(8) Edward m. * 8 Nov. 1676 Mrs. Susan Richard.

(9) James of the parish of Holy Cross, Worcestershire, m. † 21 Apl. 1796, by licence, Margaret Rodda of Penzance, and had by her Sarah and Samuel, bapt. † 4 Feb. 1810, and Mary Anne, bapt. † 8 Sep. 1811.

(10) Nathaniel Beard of Exeter, B.A. Ex. Coll. 14 Oct. 1697, Vicar of Tavistock 1701-30, bur. 24 Dec. 1730, had four children—

i Nathaniel, surgeon, b. and bap. 9 Jan. 1721, J.P. 1761, Portreeve of Tavistock 1772, m. ? Ann Spilman, their dau. Catherine m. William Halliday of Gloucester.

ii Richard had four children, John, Richard, Martha, Mary. John's children were Richard and Rebecca.

iii Catherine m. 12 Nov. 1740 William Rowe

iv Frances.

(11) Mrs. Catherine Beard m. Mr. Arthur Harris 1579 at Ludgvan.

(12) George Beard, fellow of Exeter College, Oxford, 30 June 1614, d. 20 Oct. 1638.

BODINNAR, *see* TONKIN.

BOSON OF PAUL AND MADRON.

William Boson of Paul had three sons (1) Nicholas, (2) William (3) Arthur.

(1) Nicholas, bapt. Paul 25 Mch. 1596, m. * 29 Jan. 161$\frac{3}{4}$ Alse Besvarges, and had by her (i) William, (ii) Nicholas. (iii) Mary. (An Alse Boson m. * 18 June 1634 John Haime.)

i William, bapt. Paul 24 May 1634.

ii Nicholas, who m. and had issue 1, Nicholas, 2, John, 3, Benjamin, 1, Catherine, 2, Mary.

1 Nicholas, bapt. Paul 11 Aug. 1653, d. 22 Apl. 1703, his son William was bur. Paul 2 Dec. 1695.

2 John, bapt. Paul 29 Mch. 1655, ? bur. Paul 5 May 1719. Mr. John Boson was the author of some writings in the Cornish language. *See* "Bibliotheca Cornubiensis" i. 38, 200.

3 Benjamin, b. Paul 22 Feb. 166$\frac{4}{5}$.

1 Catherine, b. Paul 26 Mch 1657, m. Ludgvan 15 Sep. 1680, Aaron Atkins of Exeter, merchant.

2 Mary, b. Paul 2 Dec. 1659.

iii Mary, bapt. 15 Sep. 1631.

(2) William, bapt. Paul 28 Feb. 160$\frac{0}{1}$.

(3) Arthur, bapt. Paul 7 Apl. 1603, m. Paul 14 Nov. 1631, Blanch, and had by her Thomas, bapt. Paul 30 Apl. 1635; Arthur, bapt. Paul 25 Apl. 1639; William, bapt. Paul Mch. 1641; Elizabeth, bapt. Paul 9 Dec. 1632.

There were other families of the same name, *e.g.*

(A) George Boson of Paul, who m. and had issue Thomas, Jane, Margaret and Juliana.

i Thomas bapt. Paul 8 Dec. 1649, and who probably was bur. 5 May 1719. It is thought that he had a dau. Blanch bapt. Paul 15 Mch. 167$\frac{5}{6}$, who m. Paul 23 Feb. 171$\frac{1}{2}$ William Bunbury, gentleman.

i Jane bapt. 7 Mch. 165$\frac{2}{3}$.

li Margaret bapt. 21 Sep. 1642, m. Paul 29 Jan. 167½
Richard Noye.

iii Juliana bapt. Paul 27 May 1651. A Juliana probably the same person m. Paul 30 Apl. 1686 John Bowes of Tredavo in Paul, and was bur. Paul 12 Nov. 1717.

(B) Thomas Boson m. Paul 8 Aug. 1632 Elizabeth Grosse ?.

Ursella Boson m. Paul 28 Oct. 1610 Nicholas Newhall.

Joan Boson m. Paul 15 Oct. 1621 William Simon.

Elizabeth dau. of Richard Boson, bapt. Paul 18 Apl. 1633.

Catherine Boson of Paul, m. Paul 12 June 1694 John Perry (?) of Ludgvan.

(C) Bartram Boson of Madron, gentleman, m. Amy, who was a widow in 1704, and had by her—
i. Jonathan b. Madron 24 Sep. 1685.
ii Bartram b. Madron 9 Nov. 1689
iii Juliana b. Madron 30 Aug. 1683, m. † 29 June 1704 Edmund Barret, mariner.

COX OF DUNDEE.

James Cox of Dundee m. Helen Scott, and d. Lochee, near Dundee, leaving eight sons and one daughter.

(1) James, m. Clementina Carmichael, and had issue ten children, of whom five survive. Resides at Clement Park.

(2) David d. unmarried.

(3) William m. Liff 23 Feb. 1813, m. (1) Robina, dau. of David Methven, who d 1862? leaving one dau. Florence b. Lochee 12 Mch. 1856; m. (2) at Claverhouse, Dundee, 21 June 1864 Elizabeth second dau. of H. S. Boase, F.R.S, b. Penzance 25 July 1831, privately bapt. by Rev. Geo. Morris, and has—
i William Henry b. Foggilcy, Lochee, 14 Apl. 1865.
ii Arthur James b. Foggiley 8 Apl. 1866.
iii Albert Edward b. Foggiley 21 Mch. 1868.
i Annie Elizabeth b. Foggiley 24 Feb. 1870.
ii Rosamond Jane Maria b. Foggiley 2 Nov. 1872.

(4) Robert m. in Canada, and has one son.

(5) Henry m. Anne Preston and has one daughter.

(6) Thomas H. m. Adelaide dau. of Mr. Galloway and widow of Mr. Brown; no issue. Resides at Duncarse.

(7) George A. m. Eliza Methven who d. 1873: issue six sons and one daughter. Resides at Beechwood, Lochee.

(8) Edward who. d. young.

(9) Ellen m. David Methven who d. leaving by her three sons.

James, William, Thomas H., and George Cox above mentioned constitute the firm of Cox Brothers, Flax and jute spinners, power loom linen and jute carpet manufacturers, bleachers, dyers and calenderers at Camperdown Linen Works, Lochee, Dundee. Mr. Cox who d. 1741 was one of the first persons to make experiments in the use of jute. The Camperdown Linen Works, which were built 1845-50, stand on 18 acres of land, contain 1000 looms, and employ about 4700 hands. This is almost the only establishment where the processes of spinning, bleaching, dyeing, weaving, printing, calendering and packing are carried on in the same locality. The steam for the engines is generated by 22 boilers, and the smoke from the furnaces is carried off by an ornamental chimney stack 300 feet high and 35 feet in diameter at the base. See " The Industries of Scotland. By David Brenmer" (1869), pp. 262-65.

DAVIES OF BURIAN.

HENRY DAVIES of Burnuhall in Burian was bur. Burian 30 May 1744, m. Hester, dau. and coheiress of Humphry Noye, she was bur. Burian 10 Apl. 1740. The issue were:
(1) William m. Elizabeth Harvey 22 Jan. 1709.
(2) Christopher of Burnuhall bur. Burian 6 Apl. 1742. By a first wife he had Henry bur. 11 Apl. 1742 ?; and Elizabeth who m. Henry Bennet of Penzance. Christopher Davies m. secondly 30 Apl. 1720 Isabel dau. of Richard Pearce of Paul. She was bur. Burian 1 June 1725. The issue were—
i James.
ii Humphry.
iii George.
iv Ann, d. unm.
v Juliana d. 1801, m. 1750 Edward Nicholas of Perranuthno, son of Hen. Nicholas of St. Hilary.
vi Margaret.
vii Isabel.
(3) John.
(4) Humphry.
(5) Hester.
(6) Ann.
(7) Mary m. Henry Foot.
William Davies of Tredrea, St. Erth, b. 1637, d. 1691, m. 21 July 1679 Catherine d. of Humphry Noye, she d. June 1714. His children were—
(1) Henry, b. 1682, d. Oct. 1737.
(1) Catherine, b. 6 Jan. 1725, d. Tredrea 3 Feb. 1803, m. Edward Giddy, Rector of St. Erth, b. 5 Sep. 1734, d. 6 March 1814.
(2) Mary, d. 2 Jan. 1740.
(3) Philippa, d. 18 Aug. 1755.

GLASSON OF PAUL.

JOHN GLASSON was bur. * 22 Jan. 1799, aged 72. Ho m. Jane, bur. * 6 Aug. 1792 and had by her—
(1) John bapt.* 16 Feb. 1755.
(2) George of Alwyn in Paul bapt. * 15 May 1757, bur. in Paul Church 26 Nov. 1802, m. * 15 June 1780 Sarah dau. of Richard Boase (witnesses Richard Boase, John Glasson). She was bapt. * 28 Jan. 1760, bur. * 2 Dec. 1802. The issue were—
i John b. * 15 Oct. 1782.
ii George Boase, Surgeon, R.N., 21 May 1813, M.D. Exeter and Plymouth, d. Meare 7 Feb. 1857 age 74, m. Stoke 30 May 1822, eld. dau. of Thomas Husband, banker, Devonport, and had by her Cordelia, who m. Stoke 7 Oct. 1851, Fred. W. White. V. of Meare, Somerset; V. of Crowle, Linc. 1868.
iii Richard Boase bapt. * 9 June 1792, bur. 29 July.
i Sarah Boase bapt. * 18 Feb. 1784, m. ? Glasson.
ii Hester bapt. * 30 July 1785, m. Tarraway of Devonport.
iii Jane m. Eady.
iv Elizabeth bapt. * 20 July 1788, m. Simmons, a master R.N.
v Phillis Boase bapt. * 17 May 1795.
vi Elizabeth Boase bapt. * 23 Feb. 1798.
Other Glassons occur at Madron, and about 1600 one of them m. Elizabeth dau. of John Levelis Esq.

HOSKING OF LANDITHY IN MADRON.

Thomas Hosking came from Brannion in Lelant to Landithy in Madron, and d. † 22 Apl. 1769, aged 76. He

m. (1720 ?) Jane dau. of Edmund Paull of Gulval. She d. †
10 July 1772, aged 75. Their children were—
(1) Ann who m. Wallis, and had by him Christopher;
Nicholas; Thomas; John; Elizabeth m. Bullock;
Ann, m. † 26 Apl. 1771 William Penrose of Penzance,
witness Mary Penrose; Mary; Jane, m. Thomas
Leggoe.
(2) Christopher.
(3) Mary, bur. † 30 May 1726, in her first year.
(4) Mary, m. † 15 Aug. 1754 her cousin Capt. Richard
Hosking of Uny Lelant, (witness, John Hosking) and
had by him Thomas, who d. at Penzance about 1837.
Thomas Hosking gave in 1833 eighty pounds to John
Batten, Esq., Mr. James Glasson, Capt. Giddy, R.N.,
and the Churchwardens and overseers for the time
being of the parish of Madron, in trust for the purpose
of giving a dinner (the expense of which shall not
exceed four pounds) annually to the inmates of the
Poor-house in the parish, on the 10th Feb., being his
birthday.
(5) Thomas.
(6) Jane, m. James Glasson, 1760 ?
(7) Elizabeth, m. † 18 May 1761 William Vinicombe.
(8) Son, who d. abroad.
(9) John, m. 17 Jan. 1770, Jane dau. of Johns of Helston, and had by her—
i Thomas, in orders, b. 7 Oct. 1772, m. Ann Blount of
Notts, and had two sons and four daughters,
ii John, b. 8 Apl. 1776, m. 29 May 1807, Jane dau. of
Thomas Polkinhorne of Perranuthno, who d. 3 Apl.
1862, and had by her, 1 John of Marazion, b. May
1815; 2 Richard, b. 17 Nov. 1830, educated at St.
Bartholomew's Hospital. M.R.C.S. England, and
L.S.A. 1852, Surgeon of Penzance Public Dispensary
21 Apl. 1869; 3 Mary Paul Johns.
i Jane, b. 6 Dec. 1770, d. unm.
ii Mary, b. 24 May 1774, d. unm.
iii Elizabeth Johns, b. 15 Apl. 1778, d. 3 Jan. 1779.

LEY OF PENZANCE.

GEORGE LEY of Penzance m. 9 July 1691 Jane second
dau. of Eliasaph Daniel, and thus obtained the Lariggan
estate, a portion of the manor of Alverton. She was b. 21
Mch. 1672, and d. 17 Feb. 1698. The issue of this marriage
were—
(1) Jane b. 16 Feb. 1693, d. 9 Jan. 1705.
(2) Grace b. 19 Jan. 1691.
(1) George b. 28 Dec. 1697, d. 12 Oct. 1776, m. 17 Aug.
1753 Catherine dau. of Joseph Beard of Halwin by his
first cousin, a dau. of the Rev. — Beard. She was b.
1720 and d. 11 Jan. 1778. The issue were—
i Daniel b. Penzance 16 Apl. 1754, bapt. 19 Apl., d. 24
Sep. 1806, m. Madron 28 Sep. 1781 Alice Bodilly,
who d. 4 Nov. 1831, aged 77. leaving no issue.
ii George b. 31 Oct. 1755, killed in the campaign of
Seringapatam 1799.
iii John b. 3 Apl. 1759, bapt. 8 June, d. unmarried in
the West Indies.
i Catherine b. 22 June 1757, bapt. 29 July, d. The
Terrace, Market-Jew street, Penzance, 29 Jan. 1833,
monu. St. Mary's Churchyard. "The last of her
family."

George Ley of Penzance occurs as having the following
children (perhaps a first marriage of the George Ley, who
m. 1753 Catherine Beard)—
(1) Daniel Trethewy, bapt. Penzance, 6 Aug. 1721, bur.
Penzance 7 Nov. 1723.

(2) Jennifer, bapt. Penzance 15 Jan. 1722, bur. Penzance
17 Oct. 1723.
(3) Elizabeth, bapt. Penzance, 9 Oct. 1724.
(4) John, bapt. Penzance 10 Oct. 1731.
(5) Joseph, bapt. Penzance 27 July 1733.

George Ley of Tavistock was at Exeter Coll. Oxf. 30
Mch. 1674—80 Oct. 1677. It is possible that this is the
George Ley mentioned above, who m. 1691 Jane Daniel.
Samuel Ley, gent., d. 1906, and has a monument in Mad-
ron Church.

LUGG OF ST. KEVERN AND PENZANCE.

GEORGE LUGG of St. Kevern m. ? 1684 Jane James, and
had by her Thomas, Simon, Henry, George, Alexander.
(1) Thomas b. 1685, m., and had James; Thomas who m.
Elizabeth Lugg; Jane who m. Penticost; and Mary.
(2) Simon b. 1687, m., but had no issue.
(3) Henry of Madron, b. 1688, d. circa 1770, m. at Gulval
8 Oct. 1719 Ann d. of Edmund Paull of Gulval, and
had by her George, Henry, John, Jane, and two
children who d. infants.
1. George of Madron, b. 1723, m. 19 July 1756 Jane
Stevens of Madron (witn. John Sampson, Henry
Lugg), and had by her—
i Elizabeth bap. 14 Aug. 1757.
ii Henry bap. Gulval 18 Oct. 1759.
2, Henry b. 1725, m. Jane Sampson, and had by
her James, Henry, Elizabeth, Phillis.
i James bap. 18 Feb. 1759.
ii Henry.
i Elizabeth.
ii Phillis bap. Madron 29 Sep. 1757.
3. John m. and had 4 sons and 2 daughters.
1. Jane bap. Madron 17 Feb. 1734, d. 12 Jan. 1821,
bur. St. Mary's, Penzance, 17 Jan., m. at Madron 27
Ap. 1756 Arthur Boase.
(4) George b. 1690.
(5) Alexander b. 1692.

LUKE OF MADRON AND PAUL.

(1) Robert Luke of Madron was bur † 20 Jan. 1625.
("'Mr. Robert Luke' bur. † 4 Oct. 1637"): he m.
Elizabeth bur. † 6 Dec. 1614, 'wife of Robert Luke.'
Their children were—
1. John bur. † 27 May 1589.
2. Jermyn bap. † 30 Nov. 1592, bur. † 30 Sep. 1648,
m. † 8 Apl. 1616 Ann, and had by her
i John bap. † 18 Apl. 1616.
ii Robert bur. † 17 Feb. 1624.
iii Mary bur. † 21 Feb. 1624.
iv Robert bap. † 20 Oct. 1626.
v Ann bur. † 7 Nov. 1647.
3. Alice bap. † 28 Sep. 1597.
4. Agnes bap. † 22 March 1602.
5. Thomas bur. † 7 Aug. 1608.
(2) John bur. † 11 Apl. 1651, 'John senior,' m. † 25 Jan
1601 Jane, bur † 26 Dec. 1656 widow; issue
1. Thomas bap † 10 Dec. 1609, bur. † 13 Dec.
2. John bap. † 17 March 1611.
3. John bap. † 27 Oct. 1616, m. † 11 Nov. 1648 Margaret, bur. † 29 Nov. 1675, and had by her
i Charles bap. † 25 Feb. 1645, bur. † 18 Apl 1649.
ii Cicely b. † 12 Aug. 1656, bur. † 28 Aug.
iii Charles bap. † 20 Sep. 1661, bur. † 4 Apl. 1664.
iv John bur. † 6 Sep. 1662.

1. Pascaw bap. † 5 Apl. 1602.
2. A dau. bap. † 8 July 1604.
3. Jane m. † 20 Jan. 163⅔ Thomas Sleepe,
4. Juliana m. † 25 Ap. 1640 Henry Pascoe.
(3) Thomas bur. † 4 Nov. 1596, had a dau. Elizabeth bap.
   † 8 Oct. 1592.
(4) William bur. † 7 July 1667, m. (1) † 10 Feb. 163⅔
   Dorothy, m. (2) Jane, m. (3) † Aug. 1656 Ann, bur. †
   28 May 1676. His children were
   1. William bap. 18 Jan. 164⅔ Gulval, 'son of William
      of Penzance.' ? m. * 25 Nov. 1676 Ana Tonken.
      Jane wife of William was bur. 22 Sep. 1655 Ludgvan,
      their child Matthew was born 21 Sep., bap. 22 Sep.
      1655.
   2. Stephen bap. † 5 Nov. 1648, his son William was
      bap. † 20 Ap. 1673, and bur. † 24 Mch. 167⅔.
(5) Stephen m. † 18 Feb. 1753 Margaret dau. of John
   Trewavas of Penzance, and cousin of Henry Boase,
   banker, bap. 14 July 1721, living 1779, and had by her
   1. A dau. who m. Mr. John.
   2. John of Newlyn bap. † 27 Feb. 1756, m. Pike, and
      was father of
      i Ann m. Joseph Batten ? 1777, he d. March 1823.
      She d. Alverton street, Penzance.
      ii John, of whom presently.
   3. Stephen, M.D. London, bap. || 4 June 1763, d. Cavendish
      square, London, 29 Mch. 1829. See Bibl. Cornub.
      i. 328.   He m. Harriet only dau. of Philip Vyvyan,
      and sister of Sir Vyel Vyvyan, and had by her
      i Rev. Francis Vyvyan, of Langdon, St. Clear near
        Liskeard, m. Agnes Eliza Ramsden, and had issue.
      ii Edward Vyvyan m. Georgiana Larkins, and had
         issue.
      iii Rev. Henry Vyvyan.
      iv Harriet Waller Vyvyan m. John M. Cannell, and
         had issue.
      v William Vyvyan m. Ann Holdsworth.
      vi Ella d. young.
      vii Mary d. young.
   John of Newlyn bur. St. Mary's, Penzance, May 1831, m.
   (1) Ann 2 dau. and coh. of Thomas Woodis of Penzance : (2) Jane dau. of Maddern of St. Just, by whom
   he had Mary, b. 1800 Penzance, d. Lifton, Devonshire.
   m. at Stythians 23 June 1840 Richard Bluett, surgeon
   of Penryn, 2nd son of Rev. Lovell Bluett of Mullion,
   and had issue two children. By his first wife John
   Luke had
   1. John of Penzance, b. 1785, d. 7 Ap. 1856, bur. St.
      Mary's, m. † 27 Apl. 1818 Mary Anna eld. dau. of
      William Morris of Oxford by Sarah Savage, who d.
      19 Ap. 1831. bur. St. Mary's, and had by her
      i John William Morris, b. 22 Sep. 1819, d. 1 Feb.
        1855, bur. St. Mary's.
      ii Henry Albert b. 30 Jan. 1827, d. || 8 July 1829,
         bur. St. Mary's.
      iii Frederic Augustus, b. 16 Nov. 1830, m. Agnes
          Kelly at New Orleans, and had by her one son,
          and a dau. Catherine Mary, b. Balaclava, bap.
          Constantinople, d. July 1856 London an infant
      i Mary Ann Charlotte b. 9 Jan. 1821, d. || 13 June
        1839, bur. St Mary's.
      ii Emily Sarah b. 30 Jan. 1823, d. † 15 May 1848,
         bur. St. Mary's.
   2. Stephen of Penzance d. Sep. 1828, bur. St. Mary's,
      m. Emma 5 dau. of John Millett of Bosavern, St.
      Just, b. 1 May 1793, d. March 1829, bur. St. Mary's,
      and had by her
      i John Millett d. at sea unm.
      ii William, captain R.N., b. || 22 Oct. 1820, lives at
         21 Cromwell Crescent, South Kensington, m.
         Georgina dau. and coh. of William Larkins of
         Kensington and Lewisham, and had by her

a Edmund William b. Sidmouth 6 Oct. 1861.
b Harriet Emma b. Cape of Good Hope 18 Jan. 1860.
c Edith Julia b. Charlton in Kent 4 July 1863.
d Annie Georgina b. Charlton in Kent 26 Ap. 1866.
e Ada Millett Raleigh b. Charlton in Kent 15
  July 1868.
f Mabel Larkins b. Devonport 6 Dec. 1871.
iii George d. Australia.
i Julia m. John Badcock Pentreath, and had three
  children, John, a son, and Julia, who m. G. W.
  Depew, he d. Peek's-rill, America, 25 July 1865,
  aged 28.
ii Mary.
iii Anne.
iv Emma d. 1863.
3. William, H.E.I.C. service, m. Mary dau. of Noah
   Brocklesby of London, she d. Bath childless.
   1. Ann Woodis d. || Jan. 1855, unm., bur. St. Mary's.
   2. Sarah d. || unm.
   3. Julia d. London, m. Capt. Thomson of Falmouth,
      and had by him William, who was drowned ;
      Charles, a surgeon ; and George in holy orders.
   4. Eliza bur. St. Mary's 1869, aged 71.
(6) Mary Luke of Kenwyn m. 28 Nov. 1763 Martin
   Sholl, officer of the Customs, Truro.
   Henry Luke m. † 11 May 1789 Jane Boase, both of
   Penzance.
   Davy Luke m. at Helston 29 Jan. 1609 Jane Hosken.
   Jane dau. of Richard Luke, bap. Helston Feb. 1611.
   Catherina, ' generosa,' bur. Helston 12 Sep. 1636.
   Elizabeth wife of John Luke, bur. † 7 Oct. 1674.
   Reginald bur. || 14 Sep. 1606.
   Ellynor bur. † 30 March 1629.
   Edmund had Margaret bap. Gulval 18 June 1699;
   Grace bap. Gulval 8 Sep. 1700 ; and Margaret bap.
   Gulval 3 Ap. 1703.

MILFORD OF TRURO.

Mr. Milford of the parish of Kea had four children, (1)
Charles, (2) Jonah, (3) James, ? (4) Mary.
(1) Charles, who resided at Kea.
(2) Jonah, manager of the Carvedras Tin Smelting
   Works, b. Kea 1735, d. Truro 11 May 1812, m. at
   Madron 1 Sep. 1763 Charlotte dau. of Joseph Beard.
   She d. Truro Vean, and was bur. 14 Feb. 1810, aged
   76. Their children were—
   1 Jonah, an assayer of tin for the Messrs. Bolitho Sons
     and Co., died Marketjew street, Penzance, unmarried.
   2 Samuel, m. Ann ? Jenkins of Redruth, and had by
     her, i Henry, ii Samuel, iii Frederick, iv Jonah Jenkin,
     i Caroline, ii Harriet, and iii Charlotte.   He d. in
     Mr. John Chester's house in the Market place, Pen-
     zance, in 183-.
     i Henry, commission agent, d. suddenly at the Globe
       Hotel, Plymouth, m. firstly, Emily Whitley, by
       whom he had a dau. Margaret Anne, who m. Alfred
       Miles Speer. H. Milford m. secondly Charlotte
       Ashwin and had issue a son Henry, who m the
       dau. of Stanley Lucas.
     ii Samuel, who d. Truro, m. Isabella dau. of Edward
        Dudd ; their dau. Isabella d. in infancy.
     iii Frederick, b. July 1611, d. unmarried.
     iv Jonah Jenkin Milford, iron agent, 24, Austin
        Friars and 21 Princes Square, London, formerly of
        14, Tavistock square, b. 17 Dec. 1814, m. 10 May
        1842 Elizabeth, dau. of Edward Budd of Truro,
        and had by her Edward Budd, b. 1847, d. 1848;
        Frederick, b. March 1852; Frances b. 1845; and
        Emily, born 27 June 1843, Truro, who m. (1)

Ap. 1865 Bernard Augustus Hewitt ; she m. (2)
at St. Stephen's, Paddington, 8 Feb. 1876, Russell
P. third son of the late John Russell Colvin.
i Caroline d. 3 Dec. 1874, aged 69, m. Kenwyn 16
June 1830 William Henry Bullmore, M.D., Mayor
of Truro 1839, Surgeon of the Royal Cornwall
Miners Militia for seventeen years, d. Princes'
street, bur. S. Mary's burying ground, Truro,
5 Oct. 1863, aged 63. Their children were
1. William Henry, a surgeon, d. 2 Sep. 1873, m.
30 Aug. 1860 Elizabeth, eldest dau. of Henry
Baird of Sydney, New South Wales; 2. Frederick
a sailor m. 12 Sep. 1860 Mary Taylder dau. of Dr.
Nicholas of Trevarth, Gwennap ; 3. Richard
Taunton b. Truro 6 Nov. 1838, d. Truro, 12 Sep.
1812 ; 4. Mary m. St. Luke's Chelsea, 13 Aug.
1860 Charles Percy, only son of Frederick Richards,
M.D., Berners street, London ; 5. Caroline Ann m.
at All Saints' Church, Camberwell, 14 Jan. 1873
W. Nevill. youngest son of J. T. Naukivell of
Truro ; 6. Ellen m. St. Mary's, Truro, 16 Oct.
1860 Henry Hanswell, only son of Henry Hanswell
Fishwick, Brown Hill, Rochdale. Henry Hanswell Fishwick, F.S.A., who m. Ellen Bullmore, is
the author of "The history of the parochial
chapelry of Goosnargh in the county of Lancaster,
1871 ;" "The history of the parish of Kirkham,"
1874 ; "The Lancashire Library," 1875.
ii Harriet b. 22 Nov. 1806, m. 26 July 1831 Robert
Tweedy. See Tweedy.
iii Charlotte B. b. Truro 4 May 1810, m. Truro 2
July 1839 Edwin Hornblower, second son of
William Cock of Redruth, and has issue, 1 Emma
b. Redruth 19 May 1840, m. Redruth 1862 her
cousin Samuel Abbott, assayer, Redruth, and has
issue Frederick William b. 1863, Samuel Milford
b. 1864, John Ernest b. 1866, and Francis Edwin
b. 1874 ; 2 Kate b. 1811, m. Redruth 1865 Mr.
Woods, manager of the London and South Western
Bank at ————, and has issue Charlotte Emma
b. 1866 and Mabel Kate b. 1867 ; 3 Edwin
Milford b. 1845.
1. Mary Beard b. 27 Jan. 1765, bapt. St. Mary's,
Truro, 8 (36) Mar., d. Market-jew street, Penzance, 15
Apl. 1846, m. 5 Feb. 1789 Robert Sholl. See Sholl.
2. Charlotte d. Bridport, Dorset, 1839, where is monu.
in churchyard.
3. Hannah, b. 1776 d. Ferris Town, Truro, 1834, m.
St. Clement's, May 1805 William son of Peter
Traer, b. 1775, d. 1848. Their children were
i Peter Green, b. 1807, m. Kenwyn 1835 Loveday
Croggan Jordan, who d. Aug. 1868. Their children were 1. Hannah Pinder, b. 1836, m. Liverpool
1862 Howard son of General Marshall of Plymouth.
2. Lucy Leonora b. 1838, m. Jan. 1862 Charles son
of Capt. Gardner of Birkenhead. 3. John Jordan
b. 1842.
ii William Augustus b. 1814, d. 1841.
iii Edwin Adolphus b. 1816.
i Hannah Milford b. 10 May 1806, d. 6 Mch. 1870.
ii Emma Milford, b. 10 Mch. 1810, d. 22 Sep. 1870.
iii Charlotte b. 1811, d. 28 Dec. 1857.
iv. Jane b. 18 Nov. 1818, and now (Apl. 1876) resident at Grampound.
4. Frances d. Union Terrace, Truro, 1 June 1842, bur.
Cemetery 4 June.
(3) James?
(4) Mary.
This family bears the same arms as the Milfords of Exeter.

MILLETT OF MARAZION

Leonard Millett (? son of James, Mayor of Marazion
1652, 1654, 1657, bur. 17 March 1688 St. Hilary : and ?
brother of Humphry and Martin), Mayor of Marazion 1675,
1680, ? d. 1686 (inventory dated 22 April 1686), had a son
Robert, said to have been secretary to Sir Cloudesley Shovel,
and who perished with him in the wreck of the English
fleet off Scilly 22 Oct. 1707. By his wife Margaret Oke,
Robert left a son Leonard, who was Mayor of Marazion
1721, and died 1740. He married (1) in 1716 June d. of
John Millett of Gurlyn in S. Erth, and (2) 8 June 1731, at
S. Just in Penwith, Grace, who d. 1757. His children by
the second marriage were—
(1) Humphry, d.] 3 June 1757, m. Elizabeth dau. of
Adams by Ustick of St. Just, who d. || 9 June 1757,
and had by her—
  1 Jane, m. Henry Sampson of Penzance, but died childless.
  2 Humphry, d. unm.
  3 Grace, d. || Sept. 1826, age 76, m. 1776 Robert, son of
  Edmund Davy, who d. 1794, age 48. Their eldest
  son was Sir Humphry Davy, the great chemist, born
  || 17 Dec. 1778 ; the second son Dr. John Davy, born
  || 24 May 1790.
  4 Leonard, d. unm.
  5 Elizabeth, born 1754, d. 19 Dec. 1820, bur. S.
  Hilary, m. 27 July 1796 her first cousin Leonard
  Millett, but d. childless.
(2) Robert, d. 26 Sept. 1809, m. Anna Tresidder, who d.
12 March 1793, age 65, and had by her—
  1 Leonard, b. 1753, d. 15 March 1841 (tablets in Marazion
  and St. Hilary Churches) m. 27 July 1796 his first
  cousin Elizabeth.
  2 Robert, Mayor of Marazion 1790, d. Marazion 22
  March 1819, age 62, m. Mary Hockin of Pool in
  Illogan, and had by her, Robert, Mary, Grace, Ann,
  Hannah, Elizabeth.
  3 John of Truro, d. Marazion 24 Sept. 1836, aged 77,
  m. 2 Jan. 1791 Mary James of Constantine, neice
  Boulderson. Their son John, lieutenant R.N.,
  m. Madron 25 Aug. 1817, Elizabeth sister of Sir
  Humphry Davy, who d. 16 Aug. 1839.
  4 Anna, d. unm.
  5 Grace, d. unm.
(3) George of Helston, d. 26 March 1781, m. 4 Feb. 1752
Ann, only d. of Sampson Sandys, b. 1724, d. 26 (? 29)
March 1806, and had by her Leonard, George, Sampson, Leonard, William, John, James, James, Ann,
Jane.
(4) William, m. Ann Barnes, d. childless.
(5) James of Helston, m. at Helston 23 April 1752 June
Nicholls, and had by her—
  1 Grace, d. under age of 20
  2 James.
  3 James.
  4 John of Padstow, m. Ursula White, d. childless.
  5 William.
  6 William, lieut. R.N., d. 12 Jan. 1821, age 58, bur. S.
  Mary's churchyard, Penzance.
  7 Humphry, d. in India.
  8 Jane.
  9 Jane, b. 1769, d. Falmouth 16 Feb. 1861, bur. S.
  Mary's churchyard, Penzance, m. 16 July 1795 John
  Bonse, born † 24 Feb. 1771, bap. † 2 April, d. || 23
  March, and bur. 27 March 1850.
(6) John, d. inf.
(7) Leonard, d. inf.
(8) Jane, d. inf.
Peter Millett was one of the twelve chief inhabitants of
Marazion mentioned in the Charter of 1595.

D

This account of the Millett family is only worked out so far as to shew the descent of Jane who married John Boase.

OXENHAM (OR OXNAM) OF PENZANCE.

RICHARD OXENHAM or OXNAM is said to have come to Penzance from Newlyn East, where his father is reported to have impoverished himself by too great a devotion to field sports. Richard was at first in the employment of Messrs. Batten and Co., but afterwards a prosperous merchant in business on his own account. He d. Penzance 25 Apl. 1793, monument in St. Mary's. He. m. Paul 30 May 1763 Elizabeth dau. of [William ?] Bodinnar of Chune in Paul. She was bapt. 24 Feb. 1745. Her sister m. Mr. (? John) Batten. R. Oxenham's children were (1) Thomas, (2) Richard, (3) William, (4) James, (1) Elizabeth, (2) Anne, (3) Mary.

(1) Thomas bapt. Penzance 5 Mch. 1765.
(2) Richard b. 20 Dec. 1768, bapt. Penzance 27 Jan. 1769. A merchant, built Rosehill, Penzance. He gave in 1793 £5 per an. out of the Rosehill estate to the poor of Madron. Sheriff of Cornwall 1810, d. Wellington terrace, Penzance, 23 Aug. 1814, m. 12 Aug. 1794 Mary dau. of Mr. John, who d. Penzance 5 July 1812, aged 45, monu. Madron Church.
(3) William of whom hereafter.
(4) James bapt. Penzance 1 May 1772, d. unm. at sea 1794 ?.
(1) Elizabeth, b. || 4 Sep. bap. || 16 Sep. 1765, d. 23 March 1801, m. † 9 Jan. 1792 John Jones Pearce of Burian; witnesses, Richard Oxnam, James Pearce.
(2) Anne bapt. Penzance 12 Mar. 1767. d. 1801 ?, m. Mr. Unwin, and had issue a girl who d. in infancy.
(3) Mary b. 22 Apl. 1778, d. Penzance, 3 Mch. 1855. She m. 16 Oct. 1800 John second son of Joshua Jepson Oddy of Darnell, Attercliffe, Yorkshire, a Russian merchant in business in London as J. Oddy and Co. He was h. 9 July 1778, and d. 12 Dec. 1832. The issue were John h. 19 June 1802, d. Blackheath, Kent. 30 Nov. 1823, and Mary Oxenham b. 21 Dec. 1803, now (Apl. 1876) living at 9, Victoria place, Penzance.

The REV. WILLIAM OXENHAM, third son of Richard Oxenham, was h. Chapel street, Penzance, 18 Dec. 1771. Of Oriel Coll., Oxf., B.A. 4 Mar. 1794, M.A. 14 June 1798. C. of Paul 1796-1803; R. of St. Petrock's, Exeter, 1803-44; Prebendary of Exeter 1803-44; V. of Cornwood 1824-44; d. Cornwood 23 Feb. 1844. m. (1) 13 June 1796 Elizabeth Trewecke, who was b. 8 Nov. 1776, d. in childbirth 24 Feb. 1797, bur. Paul Church 28 Feb.; Mary Elizabeth the only child by this m. was b. Paul 24 Feb., bapt. 28 Feb. 1797, d. unm. 13 Dec. 1841.
The Rev. W. Oxenham m. (2) 1798 Anne dau. of Geo. Nutcombe Nutcombe (formerly George Nutcombe Quicke), Chancellor of Exeter, by a daughter of George Lavington, Bishop of Exeter. She was b. 25 May 1773, d. Exeter 27 Oct. 1864, bur. St. David's Churchyard, and gave birth to (1) George Nutcombe, (2) William, (3) Richard, (4) Nutcombe, (1) Jane Mary, (2) Frances Maria, (3) Anne Dorothea, (4) Caroline.
(1) George Nutcombe b. 17 Nov. and bapt, Paul 17 Dec. 1799. Of Wadham Coll. B.A. 24 May 1820. Of Exeter Coll. M.A. 13 June 1823 and Fellow 1820-30; of Lincoln's Inn Barrister-at-law 22 Nov. 1825; d. 17 Earl's Terrace, Kensington West, 15 Dec. 1873, bur. Brompton cemetery, 22 Dec., memorial window in St. Philip's Church, Earl's court road, Kensington. He m. (1) May 1830 Caroline eld. dau. of the Rev. Warwick Young Churchill Hunt, D.D., V. of Bickleigh

near Plymouth, she d. Kensington 10 Dec. 1849, bur. Bickleigh. The issue were—
i George Lavington b. Plymouth 11 Aug. 1836, d. Plymouth 26 Oct. 1843, bur. Cornwood.
ii Caroline Nutcombe b. Plymouth 14 Feb. 1835, d. Kensington 8 Feb. 1867, bur. Littleworth, near Farringdon, Berks.
Geo. Nutcombe m. (2) Hamburg 1852, Mary Emma b. 1816, sister of his first wife, she d. Kensington 18 Dec. 1854, bur. Brompton cemetery, leaving one dau. Mary Elizabeth b. 1 Dec. 1854.
Geo. Nutcombe m. (3) 7 Jan. 1858, Charlotte Ellis sixth dau. of John Milligen Seppings of Culver House, Chudleigh. She was b. 2 Mch. 1822.
(2) William h. 13 Dec. 1800, bapt. Paul 27 Jan. 1801; of Wadham Coll, B.A. 21 May 1823, M.A. 17 May 1826; Assistant Master Harrow School 1826, and Lower Master 1841, d. Reigate 13 Oct. 1863, bur. at Harrow 20 Oct., m. (1) Mary dau. of Rev. Thomas Carter, Fellow and Vice-Provost of Eton College 1826. She d. 14 May 1833, bur. Harrow Church-yard, by whom he had—
i Henry Nutcombe, b. Harrow 15 Nov. 1829, bapt. Eton College 8 Jan. 1830, Scholar of Balliol Coll. D.A. 5 Dec. 1850, M.A. 1854, ordained in the Church of England 1853, C. of Wornall. Bucks, 1854, C. of St. Bartholomew's, Cripplegate, 1857, but soon after joined the Church of Rome: is the author of numerous works.
ii Frances Mary, b. Eton 8 Jan. 1828, became a member of the Church of Rome, d. 2 Aug. 1870, bur. Chiselhurst, Kent. where is monu.
The Rev. Will. Oxenham m. (2) 9 Apl. 1840, Rachel Charlotte dau. of Mr. Gray of Wembley Park, near Harrow, liv. 1876 Nutcombe House, Weybridge, Surrey. Their children are—
i Edward Lavington b. 30 Sep. 1843, educated at Harrow. Passed an examination before the Civil Service Commissioners and obtained an honorary certificate 23 July 1866; was appointed a Student Interpreter in China 28 July 1866; a 3rd Class Assistant 26 Jan. 1872; and a 1st Class Assistant 27 Sep. 1873.
ii Geo. William b. 12 May 1849, educated at Harrow, of Exeter Coll. Oxf., and Sarum Theological College 1871; C. of Holy Trinity, Sneyd, near Burslem, 1873-75; C. of Coatham and in charge of new district of Warrenby in the parish of Coatham, Yorkshire, 1875; C. of Staveley, Staffordshire; m. 12 Jan. 1876 Katherine Blanche dau. of Joseph Walker, M.D., of Burslem.
i Edith Maria b. 12 Mar. 1843.
ii Anne Eleanor b. 12 Oct. 1847.
(3) Richard b. 12 Mch. 1805, bap. 19 Ap. d. 15 Sep. 1805.
(4) Nutcombe b. 1810, educated at Harrow School to 1828; of Oriel Coll. 1828; took au open scholarship at Trinity Coll. 1829; Devon Fellow of Exeter Coll. June 1832; C. of Upton on Severn 1833; V of Modbury with C of Brownstone, Devon, 1834; M.A. 13 Nov. 1834, M.A. 17 Dec. 1839; Preb. of Exeter 26 Jan. 1850; d. Modbury Vicarage 13 Sep. 1859, aged 49; m. 9 Jan. 1834 Jane Georgiana Gould, now deceased, by whom he had—
i Robert George, Principal of Deccan College, Poonah, India.
ii Frank Nutcombe: of Exeter Coll. B.A. 1862, M.A. 1865; C. of St. Mark. Torwood, Devon, 1864; C. of Richmond, Surrey, 1865-73; C. of St. Barnabas, Pimlico, London, 1875. Resides 95, St. George's road, Pimlico, London, S.W.
(1) Jane Mary, b. 30 Mch. 1802, bapt. Paul 11 May 1802, d. Exeter 24 Apl. 1850, bur. St. David's Churchyard.

(2) Frances Maria, b. Exeter 7 Aug. 1803, bapt. Exeter Cathedral 10 Sep. d. Cornwood 22 Apl. 1825.
(3) Anne Dorothea, b. Exeter 8 Aug. 1806, bapt. St. Petrock 6 Sep. d. Exeter 10 Sep. 1875, bur St. David's Churchyard.
(4) Caroline, b. Exeter 24 Nov. 1807. bapt. St. Petrock, 25 Feb. 1808. m. in 1832 Rev. Charles John Hume, sometime Fellow of Wadham Coll. Oxf., R. of Meon Stoke, Hants, and of Bilton Grange, Warwickhsire, and had issue—
i Charles William b. 16 Sep. 1834, bapt Meonstoke 14 Oct.
ii Francis Glynne b. 24 Dec. 1844, bapt. Feb. 1845, of Queen's Coll. Oxf., B.A. 1869, C. of St. Mary Magdalen, Hastings, 1870, m. Edith dau. of Dr. Carey of Guernsey, and had one son deceased and a dau. Elizabeth.
iii Edward Plantagenet b. 6 July 1848, bapt. Aug. Sub-Lieut. in H.M. Turret ship "Captain," lost off Cape Finisterre 7 Sep. 1870.
iv Frederick Nutcombe b. 11 Sep. 1850, bapt. Oct.
v Duncan Cospatrick b. 13 Feb. 1854, bapt. Mch.
i Mary Louisa b. 26 July 1838, bapt. Aug.
ii Anna Caroline b. 7 Jan. 1843, bapt. Feb.
iii Agnes Marion Griselda b. 28 Dec. 1846, bapt. Feb. 1847.

The members of the Oxenham family at one time called themselves Oxnam, but the original form of name was resumed about forty years ago.
John Oxnam, gent., of Newlyn East, 1811 gave a school house and garden for the education of poor children in that parish. He also endowed it with £6 5s per an. for teaching the children and for the necessary repairs of the building.
In 1843 two Acts of Parliament were passed authorising leases and setts to be granted of and in an estate in the parish of Newlyn, devised by the will of John Oxnam deceased to John Oxnam for his life.

PARKER.

MATTHEW son of William and Dora Parker of Dublin was b. Dublin 3 August 1812. He was for some time in business in Plymouth, then resided for many years at Albury, Surrey, but afterwards removed to Leamington where he still remains. He m. Budock near Falmouth 7 Nov. 1837 Laura Elizabeth fifth dau. of Henry Boase by Anne Craige. She was b. Knightsbridge, London 27 Aug. 1807, and privately bapt. by the Rev. J. Townshend. Their children are—
(1) Lewis b. Plymouth 25 Sept. 1843, bapt. St. Andrew's Church, educated at the Agricultural College at Cirencester. Emigrated to Canada and took up a grant of government land in the Township of Harberg, Canada West, where he still remains. He m. Annie Tassie, a Canadian of Scotch parentage b. 15 Sep. 1845. His children are Lewis b. 18 Mch. 1869; Florence b. 9 Feb. 1870 ; Herbert Matthew b. 1872 ; a son b. 1874.
(1) Florence b. Plymouth 16 Oct. 1842, bapt. C. A. Church, m. 8 June 1865, at C. A. Church, Southwalk, London, John eldest son of John Belcher, b. Church Street, Trinity Square, Southwark 10 July 1841. John Belcher is an architect and surveyor at 5 Adelaide place, City of London, in partnership with his father under the firm of John and John Belcher. He resides at 38 Somerleyton road, Brixton.
(2) Gertrude b. Plymouth 31 Mch 1845, bapt. St. Andrew's Church. Now resident in Birmingham.

D²

PEARCE.

WILLIAM PEARCE of Penzance, Merchant, bought Kerris in Paul of the family of Hicks. He m. Madron 6 Nov. 1663, Elizabeth Lanyon, (possibly it was his second marriage, as an entry occurs at Madron 1654, May 6, William Pearse m. Elloner, see below) and had issue—
(1) Richard, of whom presently.
(2) Leonard bapt. † 17 Sep. 1665, bur. † 22 Apl. 1666.
(3) William bapt. † 21 May 1670.
(4) Duke, in holy orders and a schoolmaster. Of Pembroke Coll. Camb. B.A. 1699, d. Paul 17 Nov. 1712, in his thirty fourth year. Monument in Madron Church.
(1) Elizabeth bapt. Madron 27 Jan. 1666-67, living in 1720. She was m. by Rev. John Penhelick, V. of Gulval, at Morvah 8 July 1709 to Rev. Thomas Rowe, V. of Madron, who d. Madron 28 Aug. 1716 in his fortieth year, and was bur. 31 Aug. Monu. Madron Church.
(2) Grace m. Rev. John Penhelick, V. of Gulval, 1700-1730, b. 1669, d. 18 Feb. 1730, without issue.
(3) Dorcas bapt. † 9 May 1679.

RICHARD PEARCE of Kerris son of Will. Pearce b. 1664 ?, m. Mary eldest dau. of John Borlase of Pendeen in St. Just by Mary Keigwin. She was bapt. 5 Dec. 1669 and d. 3 Jan. 1759-60. (She m. secondly the Rev. Henry Pendarves, V. of Paul). The issue of her first marriage were
(1) Richard, of whom presently.
(1) Elizabeth bapt. † 1 Dec. 1683. [An Elizabeth dau. of a R. Pearce m. * 30 Oct. 1708 Nicholas Keigwin.]
(2) English bapt. Madron 14 Feb. 1685-6.
(3) Mary bapt. Paul 25 Feb. 1695-6.
(4) Isabel who m. 30 Apl. 1720 Christopher Davies of Bencal in Buryan, who was bur. 6 Apl. 1742.

RICHARD PEARCE only son of R. Pearce d. 25 June 1753, aged 60. He m. firstly (Ruth) Bodinnar of Paul, who was bur. Paul 20 Oct. 1724. He m. secondly Maria dau. of Lieut.-Gen. John Jones of Penrose in Buryan, Governor of Hull. She d. Penzance 5 Apl. 1783, aged 76. R. Pearce's children were—
(1) Richard of Tredinny, Buryan, in holy orders, of Pembroke Coll. Cambridge, B.A. 1748, M.A. 1752, Curate of Sennen ? 1761. bur. Buryan 24 May 1787.
(2) John, a midshipman R.N., d. at sea.
(3) William, of whom presently.
(1) Mary d. Dec. 1803, bur. Penzance.
(2) Jane d. July 1814, aged 81, bur. Gulval.
(3) Elizabeth b. and bapt. privately at Paul 14 June 1741, d. Exeter 18 Nov. 1778. monu. at Madron. She m. at Madron 28 July 1766 John Beard junr. of Halwin in Paul, wita. Jane Pearce, Caroline Borlase.
(4) Ann d. Burley Grove near Penzance 21 Dec. 1832, aged 87, bur. Gulval.

WILLIAM PEARCE, third son of R. Pearce, was a solicitor, d. 16 Jan. 1767, aged 30, and was bur. Penzance. He m. Madron 22 Mch. 1763 Mary dau. of John Harvey of Trevoro in Sennen, great niece of General Jones. (Witnesses Elizabeth Pearce, Mary Jeffreyson). The issue were
(1) John Jones, of whom presently.
(1) Maria, b. ‖ 28 Dec. 1766, m. 1792, William Berryman of Penzance, surgeon.
John Jones, only son of Will. Pearce, was b. 1 Dec. 1765, d. Penzance, 7 Dec. 1826, bur. Burian. He m. firstly at Madron 9 June 1792, Elizabeth eldest dau. of Richard Oxnam of Penzance (witnesses Richard Oxnam, Ann Pearce). She was b. Penzance 4 Sep. 1765, bap. 16 Sep., d. Tredinner, 23 Mch. 1801, bur. Burian 27 Mch. He m. secondly, 25 Nov. 1817, Sarah dau. of Thomas Woodis of Penzance She was b. Penzance 4 May 1765. d. 4 Feb. 1841, bur. Madron. By his first wife he had—

(1) Richard, Agent to Lloyd's, Mayor of Penzance five times, b. Tredinny 22 Nov. 1792, d. Chapel-street, Penzance, 23 Aug. 1862, bur. St. Mary's Churchyard, 29 Aug., m. Truro 17 July 1826, Sarah only dau. of Henry Penneck, м n., by Sarah Pidwell. She was b. Penzance 20 Nov. 1795, d. Penzance 5 Mch. 1863. Their children were--

 i Richard Henry, b. || 22 Nov. 1832, d. || 17 May 1833.

 i Lydia Penneck b. Penzance 24 Apl. 1827 (her sponsors were Thomas Clutterbuck of Truro her great uncle, Ann Pearce her great great aunt, and Lionel Ripley her uncle). She m. 25 June 1853 Richard Quiller Couch, eldest son of Jonathan and Clara Couch, b. Polperro 12 Mch. 1817, d. Penzance 8 May 1863, by whom she had Maria Jane b. Penzance 28 May 1854; Sarah Lydia b. Penzance 21 Meh. 1856; Richard Pearce b. Penzance 25 June 1858; Margaret Quiller b. Penzance 17 March 1860.

 ii Mary Jones b. || 9 Dec. 1831, d. || 27 Jan. 1832.

 iii Margaret Gifford b. Penzance 6 Jan. 1834, d. 1834.

 iv Maria Jones (twin sister of iii) b. || 6 Jan. 1834, bap. 25 Nov. 1835, being the day of the opening of St. Mary's Church, Penzance (her sponsors were W. Arundel Harris Arundel of Lifton Park, her father's second cousin, and Mary Bennett of Bath, her grandfather Penneck's first cousin). She m. 186— James Jago, M.D. of Truro, son of John Jago. He was b. Kegilliack in Budock 18 Dec. 1815. Their children are Margaret b. Truro 1866: Jane b. Truro 1868; a son b. Truro 15 Dec. 1873, d. 19 Dec. 1873.

(2) John Jones Pearce was b. at Tredinney, Buryan. 15 Apl. 1795, entered the Royal Navy in 1801, was gazetted Lieutenant 1814, and on the conclusion of peace was placed on half pay. Being desirous of employment he took the command of the "Tulloch Castle" and traded backwards and forwards to and from the West Indies and London. From over exertion in the discharge of his duty in 1823 at Kingston, Jamaica, he fell into a consumption, from the effects of which he never recovered. In 1831 he finally left the sea, and retiring to his native county took up his residence at Burlton Castle, Newlyn. It was here during the terrible outbreak of cholera which devastated Newlyn in 1832 when so many persons ran away from the danger, that he and his wife remained at their post, aiding their neighbours by their precept and example, and administering to their wants with money, food and medicine to the utmost of their means. During the remaining months of his life he was quite an invalid, the consumptive symptoms returning with great violence. It was during one of his rides that in passing Hea Moor, Madron, he was particularly struck with a view of the mount from a plot of ground belonging to Mr. Batten. It was not long before he made up his mind on the matter. He purchased the ground, and commenced building himself a house, afterwards known as Polmenna; he did not, however, live to inhabit it, for after much suffering, he died at Burlton Castle 10 July 1833, and was interred in the burial ground at the east end of Madron Church 13 July; where a tombstone has been erected to his memory. He married Anna Maria Henrietta eldest child of Henry Boase and Anne Craige, who was b. at No. 1, Knightsbridge, London, opposite the Chapel, on Monday morning 18 Jan. 1796, and was privately bapt. by the Rev. John Townshend on Thursday 4 Feb." She was educated at the Misses Babington's School, Sloane street, Chelsea, and joined her parents at Penzance in 1811. She took a considerable share in the education of her sisters, and was for some years a companion to her father. On the 20

Nov. 1821, she was married at Madron by the Rev. George Treweeke to Lieut. John Jones Pearce, R.N. From 1825 to 1831, during her husband's voyages to the West Indies, she resided at Greenwich. A few months after his decease, she removed from Burlton Castle to Polmenna, a country house which her husband during his life had commenced building. Some time after, in 1835, she erected another house on an adjacent plot of ground. In 1836 she and her family joined the C. A. Church. She left Polmenna in 1845, and went to Dundee, first residing at No. 1, then at No. 2, Nelson street, afterwards at 57, Constitution road, and No. 2, King street. She now, 1876, lives at Eden grove, Arbroath road. In 186— she sold both her houses at Polmenna for the sum of £1600, although the land and the buildings had cost upwards of £2,500. She enjoys a Lieutenant's widow's pension from the Admiralty. Her children were—

 i John Jones b. Blackheath, Kent, 12 Oct. 1822, bap. at Lea, al. Alverne Hill, Penzance 5 Meh 1823, bur. St. Mary's churchyard.

 ii Henry Jones Pearce b. Wellington place, Penzance 14 July 1824, bap. by the Rev. M. N. Peters, at St. Mary's on the 6 Aug. He was placed under the Rev. George Morris, at the Penzance Grammar School, where he remained from 1835 to 1839. In 1840 he took a situation in the Western District Bank at Penzance and remained with that firm and with their successors Messrs. Ricketts, Enthoven. and Co. until April 1844. He then went to Dundee, where after sometime he joined Alexander Brown Glenday (previously a clerk in the Dundee Bank) in a shipping business, but this not proving profitable, he in Nov. 1848 entered the banking house of Messrs. Ransom and Co., No. 1, Pall Mall East, London. Here he got on very well, and would, if he had remained, have been high in the office, as within a very few years the whole of the staff with the one exception of Mr. Cox the cashier died or left the establishment; but hearing of a vacancy in the Dundee Bank which he thought would suit him, and being desirous of being near his mother, he left London in Sep. 1850 and joined the Dundee Bank in the same month. There he continued until 31 March 1862, when he and his brother William Alfred Pearce under the name of Pearce Bros., took over the Lillybank foundry, which W. A. Pearce had previously conducted with William Wylie Neish under a five years partnership which expired at this time. This establishment they still carry on.

 iii William Alfred Pearce was b. at Park Row, Greenwich, 13 May 1826, and bap. at St. Alphage, Greenwich, June 1826. He was educated from 1840-41. at Penair House Academy, Truro, then under the management of the late Mr. John Barwis. In 1841, he was sent to Tuckingmill and placed under the care of Mr. John Phillips to learn mechanical drawing, and at the 1842 Exhibition of the Royal Cornwall Polytechnic Society he obtained a prize for a drawing of a stationary steam engine. After this, in May 1843, he proceeded to Dundee, and there bound himself an apprentice for five years to Messrs. Kinmonds Hutton, and Steele, Wallace Foundry, where he practically learnt the business of machine making in all its various details. On the expiration of his apprenticeship, he worked as a journeyman for some months, then entered the Drawing Office of Messrs. Fawcett, Preston and Co., engineers, Liverpool, from which he obtained the situation of chief draughtsman with Messrs. Martin Samuelson and Co., Hull, where he remained a year, and then seeing no prospect of advancement or improvement he left them and went across to Caen in Normandy (where his cousins G. C. and E. L. Boase were then residing) with the intention of studying the French language, but in about two months hearing of a situation in the Drawing Office at H.M. Dockyard, Portsmouth, he returned to England and obtained the place of draughtsman at the Steam factory there. In 1857 Lilly Bank Foundry, Dundee, being to let, he in conjunction with Wm. Wylie Neish took it and entered into partnership as machine makers under the title of Pearce and Neish for five years from 31st March, at the expiration of which time the partnership was allowed to run out. On 31 Mch. 1862, he joined his brother H. J. Pearce, and under the title of Pearce Brothers, steam engine and boiler makers, millwrights, etc., the firm still continues. W. A. Pearce m. firstly at St. Paul's Dundee, 11 June 1853, his first cousin Anna Maria, eld. dau. of H. S. Boase, M.D. She was b. Chapel street, Penzance, 26 Aug. 1827, and d. Broughty Ferry, Dundee, 4 Nov. 1871. The issue of this marriage were (1) Richard. b. King street, Portsea, 15 May 1856, bap. Holy Trinity Church; (2) Lilias, b. Princes street, Dundee, 18 July 1858, bap. C. A. Church, 13 Aug.; (3) Anna Henrietta, b. Princes street, Dundee, 1 Sep. 1864, bap. C. A. Church, 7 Oct. 1864, d. Dundee, 8 Feb. 1865, bur. the Eastern cemetery. W. A. Pearce was m. secondly at Denbrae near St. Andrews, by the Rev. A. H. K. Boyd, D.D., 21 Sep. 1873. to Ann Boswall, eld. dau. of Alexander Watson Wemyss, D.D. She was b. Edinburgh, 29 Apl. 1836. The issue are (1) Elizabeth Rosa, b 1, Balgillo crescent, Broughty Ferry, 15 June 1874, bap. Episcopal Church, 31 July; (2) Harriet Evelyn, b. Broughty Ferry, 2 Nov. 1875, bap. Episcopal Church, 1 Dec.

i Anna Maria b. Park Row, Greenwich, 16 June 1828, d. Greenwich, 16 Nov. 1829, bur. St. Mary's Churchyard, Penzance.

(3) William b. 29 July 1798 d. Sierra Leone, 20 July 1813. He was a Midshipman of H M. frigate " Thais," Capt. Edward Scobell.

(4) Lionel Ripley b. Tredinny, 22 Mch. 1801 d. Jamaica 19 July 1835. He m. a widow in Liverpool.

(1) Elizabeth b. Penzance 7 June 1796 m. Francis Lugg, builder, Penzance. By a first wife F. Lugg had two sons.

The arms are 1 Pearce, 2 Jones, 3 Ripley, 4 as the first. Pearce—Az. on a fess Ar., 3 pellets between as many pelicans Or. The crest, an arm embowed in armour, holding an arrow in pale, the shaft resting on the wreath.

The following also occur at Paul: some others are added in parenthesis.—

Marriages—

1600, Nov. 9, John Pears m. Elizabeth Roben,
1608, Nov. 2, Martin Pers m. Margaret.
1618, Sep. 19, John Pears m. Florence.
1635. Aug. 18, John Pearce m. Philippa.
1640, June 8, William Pierse (?) m Mary.
(1649, Aug. 15, at St. Erth, Philippa dau. of Thomas Pearce of St. Just m. John son of John Legow of Ludgvan).
1667, Nov. 29, Phillis Pearce m. Richard Keigwin.
1670, Sep. 21, William Pearce m. Elizabeth.
(1672, Jan. 6, at Burian, John Pearce m. ——, name not legible).
1683, Oct. 29, Nicholas Pearce m. Thomasin.
1698, Ap. 30, Christian Pearce m. John Yeaman.
1699, Ap. 18. John Pearce m. Mary Nicholls.
1703, Oct. 16, John Pearce m. Margaret Cotton.

1705, Oct. 13, Mary Pearce m. William Keigwin.
1705, Nov. 17, Mary Pearce m. Bernard Yeaman, both of Paul.
1749, June 29, Honor Pearce m. Richard Keigwin.
1830, ? Ann Pearce of Newlyn m. George Glasson of Newlyn.

Baptisms—

160¼, Mch. 23, John son of John Pearce.
160½, Mch. 2, Jacob son of John Peris.
(1658, June 14, at Burian, born Elizabeth dau. of John Pearce and Tamsin, and bap. 19).
(1663, July 26, at Burian, Richard son of John Pearce and Tamzen.
(1669, Jan. 19, at Burian, Grace dau. of John Pearce and Tamzen).
1630, June 20, William son of John Pearce.
1682, Oct. 8, Jane dau. of Humfry Pearce.
1695, May 19, Nicholas son of Nicholas Pearce.
1696, Ap. 26, Catherine dau. of Humfry Pearce.
1699, May (? 7), Grace dau. of Humfry Pearce.
1699, Sep. 17, John and Jane son and dau. to Nicholas Pearce.
163?, Jan. 28, John son of John Pearce.

Burials—

1724, Oct. 20, Ruth wife of Richard Pearce, gentleman.
(172?, Feb. 22, at Burian, Abigal Pearse).
(1752, Jan. 1, at Burian. Timothy Pearce).
(1758, July 28, at Burian, Tryphena Pearce, widow).
(1759, Jan. 24, at Burian, Timothy Pearce.

The following occur at Madron :—

Marriages—

1584, Nov. 26, Richard Perse m. Elizabeth.
1589, July 13, Richard Perce m. Elizabeth.
1653, Sep. 24, Thomas Pearse m. Jone.
1654, May 6, William Pearse m. Ellonor.
1663, Nov. 6, William Pearse m. Elizabeth.
1665, June 5, Humfry Pearse m. Mary.
170? Jan. 24, Loveday Pearce of Penzance m. Alexander Reed.
1703 Oct. 6, Frances dau. of Thomas Pearce of Penzance m. Philip Carne of Gulval.
170? Jan. 1. Mary Pearce of Peuzance m. Gregory Tregurtha of Paul.
1709 Jan. 27, Timothy Pearce of S. Levan m. Tryphena Rodda of Madron.
1708 Sep. 27, John Euden m. Ann Pearce, both of Penzance.
1734, Ap. 15, Mary Pearce m. Richard Pasco, both of Madron.
1760, Dec. 23, John Pearce, Independent Minister, Penzance, m. Anne Pidwell of Penzance, witnesses, Benjamin Pidwell, Alice Pearce.
1761, Dec. 13, Susanna Pearce m. Charles Gwavas, both of Penzance, witnesses, Nicholas Pearce and Rachel Gwavas.
1765, Susanna Pearce and Charles Gwavas witness m. of John Michell and Rachel Gwavas.
1764, Sep. 30, Nicholas Pearce of Penzance m. Grace Harvey of S. Ives.
1771, Jan. 7, John Pearce m. Juliana Paull, both of Penzance, witnesses, Mary Cole, Jane Paull.

Baptisms—

1663, Aug. 13, Ellonor dau. of William Pearse.
1665, Sep. 17, Leonard son of William Pearse.
1665, Sep. 17, Thomas son of Humfry Pearse.
1666, Jan. 27, Elizabeth dau. of William Pearse.
1670, May 21, William son of William Pearce.
1679, May 9, Dorcas dau. of Mr. William Pearce.
1683, Ap. 22, William son of George Pearce.
1686, Dec. 26, Ann dau. of William Pearce.
169?, Feb. 14, Richard son of John Pearce.

Burials—

1578, Aug. 10, Jedna dau. of Symon Peres.

1578, Aug. 11, Stephen Pearcs
1578, Aug. 20, Margaret dau. of Richard Peres.
1578, Aug. 24, Jane wife of Stephen Pearcs.
1587, Mch. 30, Joane dau. of Thomas Peres.
158?, Jane 27, Elizabeth wife of Edward Peres.
1588, July 30, William son of Richard Peres.
1597, Ap. 6, the dau. of Richard Peres.
1598, Oct. 22, Richard Peres.
1604, Sep. 20, Elizabeth dau. of James Peres.
161?, Feb. 14, Joane Pears of Penzance.
1638, Nov. 16, Margaret wife of James Pears.
16⅔, Feb. 20, Katheren Pears alias Beagoe.
16⅔, Feb. 29, James Pears.
1647, July 8, Roger Pearse.
1647, July 10, Margaret Pearse.
1657, Aug. 6, Maddern Pearse.
16⅝, Jan. 9, William son of William Pearse,
1663, Aug. 13, Elloner wife of William Pearse.
1663, Sep. 2, Elloner, dau. of William Pearse.
1666, Ap. 22, Leonard son of William Pearce.
1668, Aug. 30, Humfry Pearce.
1674, Aug. 6, Jone dau. of William Pearce.
1674, Aug. 13, Jane dau. of William Pearce.
1674, Aug. 14, Jone wife of Thomas Pearce.
1677, Mch. 27, Kathrayne dau. of Thomas Pearce.
1677, Nov. 12, Richard son of George Pearce.
1679, May 13, Jone Pearce widow.
1679, July 21, son of Thomas Pearce.
(1762, Dec. 7, at Burian, Mary Pearce of Penzance.)
(1766, Feb. 21, at Ludgvan, James Perez alias Pearce.)

PAULL (PAUL) OF GULVAL.

EDMUND PAULL m. (1) 21 Jan. 1687 Jane Dunstan ; m.
(2) 3 Feb. 169? Anna Phillips. His children were Edmund,
Thomas, John, Silas, Ann, Jane.
(1) Edmund m. 1 Jan. 17?? Agatha Cara, and had by her
Edmund, Nicholas, Ann, Jane, Elizabeth.
1. Edmund m. Mary Trezise, their dau. Mary was bap.
Gulval 7 Jan. 1770.
2. Nicholas bap. 14 Oct. 1738, m. Ann Trezise.
1. Ann m. Thomas Woodis.
2. Jane m. Dillon.
3. Elizabeth bap. 26 Sep. 1730, m. John Morgan, b.
Penzance 1729.
(2) Thomas b. 2 Ap. 1704 Gulval, bap. Ap. 17.
(3) John bap. 7 Feb. 1706.
(4) Silas bap. 11 Ap. 1710, m. (1) Elizabeth Rowe, by
whom he had a dau. Ann bap. 27 Ap. 1735. He m.
(2) at Gulval 30 Ap. 1710 Charity Geach of Perran.
(1) Ann m. at Gulval 8 Oct. 1719 Henry Lugg of St.
Kevern.
(2) Jane m. Thomas Hosking of Lundithy.
The Paulls were for several generations in Gulval.
Thomas Paull, Vicar of Gulval, d. in 1660. The name
occurs still earlier in Paul and Madron. Elizabeth Paul m.
William Newton (?) 28 July 1616 at Paul. Hellen wife of
William Paul was buried 28 Ap. 1582 Madron. John Pawle
m. at Madron 21 Jan. 162⅞ Sarah. Nathaniel Paul m. † 28
Nov. 1708 Joan Bennets, both of Penzance. Juliana Paul
m. at Madron 7 Jan. 1771 John Pearce, both of Penzance
(witn. Mary Cole, Jane Paull). John Paul m. Elizabeth
Nicholls, both of Penzance, 27 May 1765 Madron, witn.
Elizabeth Nicholls. Mary Paul widow m. Stephen Crab,
both of Penzance, 13 July 1765 Madron, witn. William
Rowe.

POLLARD OF PAUL AND MADRON.

(A) The Cornish branches of this family came from
Devonshire ; one settled at Treleigh in Redruth,
another in Paul and Madron. Richard Pollard of

Horwood near Bideford, m. Margaret dau. of John
Cockworthy of Erscombe, and had by her
(1) Anthony.
(2) John m. † 31 Jan. 160¾ Elizabeth dau. and heir of
John Nevill of Trewarvenith Marchs in Paul, and had
by her Alexander of Tarevenith, who m. Jane dau. of
James Chynoweth of St. Martin's, Dieneage. Issue
Thomas, Henry, Jane, Elizabeth, and Mary.
(3) Margaret.
(4) Avice m. Walter son of John Pollard of Plymouth.
(5) Thomas.
(6) James.
(h) William Pollard was elected Fellow of Exeter
College, Oxford, 16 Feb. 1558. John and Arthur
Pollard of Redruth were at Exeter College 6 Apl. 1676
to 14 Jan. 168? and both took the B.A. degree 6 Nov 1679.
(C) James Pollard, gentleman, bur. † 18 Dec. 1606, was
father of
(1) Nicholas, bur. † 4 Aug. 1584.
(2) Elizabeth, bur. † 21 July 1585.
James Pollard, gentleman, bur. † 7 Sep. 1613.
John Pollard bur. † 11 Jan. 165⅜.
John Pollard, jun. of Madron, was father by a first
marriage, of John bap. † 16 Aug. 1646. He m. (2)
† 2 Nov. 1656 Jane, and had by her
(1) Ralph, born † 17 Feb. 165⅜, bur. † 29 May 1659.
(2) Mary, bap. † 10 Aug. 1661.
(3) Margaret, bap. † 5 Feb. 166⅔.
(D) John Pollard m. † 26 June 1708, Ann Rodda, both
of Madron, and had by her
(1) Joan, bap. † 22 May 1709, bur. † 8 Sep. 1734,
mar. † 3 Mch. 172⅔, Arthur Boase of Madron, licence
dated 20 Jan.
(2) Phillis, bap. * 21 Oct. 1721.
William Pollard of Madron, m. * 9 Feb. 171⅞, Joan
,Tremearn of Paul, and witnessed † 27 Ap. 1756, the
second marriage of Arthur Boase with Jane Lugg.
(E) James Pollard of Paul, m. † 23 Ap. 1734, Elizabeth
Williams of Penzance.
Elizabeth, servant to Mr. James Pollard, bur. † 21 Feb.
160¾.
John Pollard, m. Burian 6 June 1669 Also.
Jane Pollard, m. Burian 5 Oct. 1700, Oliver Beckerleg.

RICHARDS OF PAUL AND MADRON.

THOMAS RICHARDS m. Joan Tregortha, and had by her
Robert and William. Robert m. Rebecca, and had by her
Michael bap. * 17 Feb. 174?; William b. 19 June 1730 Pen-
hellick in St. Clements near Truro, m. (1) Jane Jordan of
St. Hilary, who d. 23 May 1753, and had by her William
b. Helston 14 May 1753, d. 30 Oct. 1807, m. Elizabeth dau.
of Hewett of Truro, who m. (2) Samuel Pidwell of Penzance. He m. (2) 26 Dec. 1758 Valentina dau. of John and
Jane Rowland, b. Ireland 22 Nov. 1735, d. 15 Ap. 1796, and
had by her
(1) John b. 11 Oct. 1759, ? d. 29 Dec. 1830.
(2) Thomas b. 19 Oct. 1761, d. ? young.
(3) George of Truro, b. 15 July 1764, d. 28 Jan. 1842,
He had two daughters Eliza and Mary.
(4) Robert of Penzance b. 9 Aug. 1766, long resident in
the West Indies as a millwright, mayor of Penzance
1830 and 1833, d. Alverton, Penzance, 11 Nov. 1848,
in his 83rd year, m. Mary Parminter of Bodriggy,
Hayle, who d. Penzance 5 Sep. 1841, aged 73.
(5) James b. 10 Aug. 1768, d. 12 Aug. 1841, m. William
Broad.
(6) Thomas b. 20 Feb. 1771, d. 18 Ap. 1862. He had a
son by his first wife, no issue by the second.
(7) Mary b. 6 Oct. 1773, m. William Stoddard, and had
by him Elizabeth Valentina, Robert, and Mary. Eliza-

beth Valentina b. Melcombe Regis, Dorset 8 Nov. 1799, m. † 11 Dec. 1824 Henry Samuel Boase, F.R.S.
(8) Elizabeth d. Penzance 20 Feb. 1862, aged 86.

SHOLL OF TRURO.

All the dates in this portion refer to Kenwyn unless otherwise stated.

RICHARD SHOLL's father is thought to have been a Richard Sholl who was bur. Kenwyn 3 Apl. 1731. Richard himself held Bosvigo in Kenwyn, which he sold to Mr. William Lemon in 1741 (Lysons' *Cornwall*, p. 158). He was bur. at Kenwyn 28 July 1745. He m. 3 Aug. 1729 Margery Nancarrow, who was bur. 21 Jan. 1795, aged about 95. She heard the death of Queen Anne proclaimed in the streets of Penryn when she was a girl of fourteen. Their children were : (1) Robert ; (2) Richard ; (3) William ; (4) Martin   (1) Mary.

(1) Robert, bapt. 23 June 1730, a Lieutenant ? R.N.
(2) Richard of Bosvigo, bapt. 26 Jan. 1734, d. 1800 ? m. (? Eleanor, bur. 25 Dec. 1811), dau. of Dunstan of Kea, and had by her : 1 Richard ; 2 Martin : 3 William ; 4 Robert ; 1 Catherine ; 2 Mary and 3 Elizabeth.
1 Richard "bapt. 6 Oct. 1766 from Kea," d. 1845 ?, m. by licence 25 Feb. 1787 Anna Maria James of Kenwyn. She was bur. 17 Nov. 1842, aged 76. The issue were i Richard, ii William, iii John, iv James, v James, i Anna Maria, ii Jane, iii Mary, iv Emma, v Clarissa.
  i Richard bapt. 31 May 1789, m. but had no issue.
  ii William bapt. 31 Jan. 1791.
  iii John bapt. C Oct. 1793.
  iv James bur. 12 Mch. 1797 an infant.
  v James bapt. 13 Sep. 1807, m. 12 Apl. 1831 Sophia Dewstoc of Kenwyn.
  i Anna Maria bapt. 16 Nov. 1797, m. by licence 29 Mch. 1830 Edward Downe of St. Clements, witness Richard Sholl.
  ii Jane bap. 21 Mch. 1800.
  iii Mary bap. 5 Sep. 1802, (?) m. by licence 25 Dec. 1821, Thomas Webber of Kenwyn.
  iv Emma bap. 16 July 1805, m. by licence 25 Dec. 1821 Horatio Nelson Tollervey of Kenwyn.
  v Clarissa bap. 16 Apl. 1811, bur. 11 Nov.
2 Martin.
3 William of St. Clements m. Miss Barnes, and had by her i William, i Elizabeth, ii Mary.
  i William of Kenwyn m. 24 July 1814 Grace Tippet of Kenwyn, and had by her
    a Henry Tippet bapt. ? Oct. 1820.
    b William bapt. 9 Oct. 1820, probably a twin.
    c Richard bapt. 1 Jan. 1824, bur. 24 July 1831, "aged 8."
    a Elizabeth Maria Tippet bapt. 8 Jan. 1816.
  i Elizabeth ? m. 27 Dec. 1845 Thomas Terrill of Kenwyn.
  ii Mary m. in London.
4 Robert bapt. 30 Nov. 1775 "from Kea."
1 Catherine bapt. 22 Sep. 1774 "from Kea."
2 Mary d. 1848, m. Thomas Lavin, farmer, St. Clements, their son Thomas d. 1842.
3 Elizabeth m. Mr. Shoebridge, their son William Shoebridge, M.D. resided in London.
(3) William, English Consul at Alexandretta. On his return to England he built Condurra near Truro. He was bapt. 14 June 1736, bur. Kenwyn 16 Dec. 1797, "from St. Clements." He m. firstly in London, and had a son Capt. William Sholl, who fell at the siege of Seringapatam in 1799. He m. secondly Maria Teresa dau. of Justo, a Greek physician at Aleppo, she d. Newton Ferrers, Devon, 24 Nov. 1833, aged 72.

Tombstone. [Cecilia Justo sister of Maria Teresa m. a cousin, and Louis Justo her brother d. in the Indian army.] William Sholl's children by this second marriage were : 1 Robert, 2 Richard, 3 Martin, 1 Mary Ann, 2 Cecilia, 3 Teresa, 4 Louisa, 5 Clara.
1 Robert b. Turkey 1781, educated at Truro grammar school, where he obtained a prize medal 1796, became a navy agent in Clement's Inn, London, and d. West Square, London, 1832. He m. Elizabeth Mutton of Plymouth, and had by her William a surgeon in Australia, Richard, Charles, Robert, and Mary who m. Capt. —— of Warwickshire.
2 Richard b. Truro 1786. "Served his country 35 years in various parts of the globe, and d. 17 Dec. 1836 in the 51st year of his age, being then Purser of the Ordinary at Chatham." Tombstone St. Mary's churchyard, Chatham. His dau. Eliza m. William Adams of Newton Ferrers.
3 Martin bapt. St. Clement's 17 Apl. 1788, d. Newton Ferrers 18 Mch. 1863. Tombstone.
1 Mary Anne b. Turkey 6 Apl. 1784.
2 Cecilia bapt. St. Clement's 3 May 1790, bur. Kenwyn 8 Mch 1797, "daughter of Mr. William Sholl from St. Clement's."
3 Teresa b. 1 Jan. 1792, bapt. St. Clement's 1 Apl., m. 1818 Alexander Penprase, purser R.N. He was b. Falmouth, and d. Newton Ferrers 22 Aug. 1869, aged 81. Tombstone.
4 Louisa b. Condurra 1794, d. 5 Windsor villas, Plymouth, 29 Oct. 1869, bur. Cemetery, m. 1821 Admiral Sir John Kingeome, K.C.B. He was b. 14 Feb. 1794, and d. 5 Windsor villas, Plymouth, 7 Aug. 1871, bur. Cemetery, will proved London 6 Feb. 1872. Their children were
  i Frederick b. Plymouth 1831, a midshipman R.N., fell overboard during the night and was lost.
  ii Louisa Teresa b. Plymouth 19 Apl. 1835, d. Exeter 22 Aug. 1865, bur. Exeter, m. Newton Ferrers Commander George Bell Williams, who d. Plymouth 18 June 1871, aged 61, and was bur. the Cemetery, where is tombstone. The issue were a Herbert b. Feb. 1858, d. Plymouth 1859 ; b Eva b. Exeter 6 Aug. ; c Charles b. Exeter 6 Aug., 1861 ; d Florence b. Exeter 2 Apl. 1863.
  iii Ellen Clara b. Newton Ferrers 26 June 1838, m. Ellis Frederick son of Rev. Henry Baugh Thorold, R. of Hougham-cum-Marston, Lincolnshire, and Julia Ellis dau. of John Thomas Ellis, M.P., of Wyddial Hall, Herts, and Mary Anne dau. of John Heaton of Bedfords, Essex. Ellis Frederick Thorold, who was b. Rauceley vicarage, Lincolnshire, Oct. 1830, was Scholar of Corpus Christi Coll. Oxf. and M.A. 1854. His medical education was obtained in Edinburgh, London, and Paris. M.D. Edinb., and M.R.C.P. Eng. 1862. Late resident surgeon Royal Maternity Hospital, Edinburgh, and consulting physician to Plymouth Provincial Dispensary, resides at 5 Windsor villas, Plymouth.
  iv and v Maitland Ferguson and Louisa Teresa, the dates of whose births have not been ascertained.
5 Clara b. Condurra 1796, d. Newton Ferrers 29 Mch. 1868, Tombstone.
(4) Martin bapt. 29 June 1739, bur. 21 Jan. 1803 ?, of H.M. Customs, Truro 1764, Tidewaiter and Searcher 16 Nov. 1769 to July 1798, m. 28 Nov. 1763 Mary Luke of Kenwyn, and had by her 1 Robert. 2 Richard, 3 William, 4 Martin, 5 John, 1 Mary, 2 Mary, 3 Elizabeth, 4 Elizabeth.
1 Robert b. 24 Oct., bapt. 3 Nov. 1765, of H.M. Customs, Truro, 1798, d. of consumption 17 Apl. 1815, m. 5 Feb. 1789 Mary Heard eldest dau. of Jonah Milford, b. 27 Jan. 1765, bapt. St. Mary's, Truro, 8 Mch., d.

Market-jew street, Penzance, 15 Apl. 1846, bur.
Independent chapel yard, where was monument, since
destroyed. Their children were i Augustus, ii William, iii Charles, iv Robert, v Jonah, i Jemima
Mary, ii Charlotte.
i Augustus, b. Boscawen street, Truro, 29 Mch. 1790,
connected with *The Courier* and *The Globe* news-
papers. d. London 16 Nov. 1862, m, Mary Bonne-
well, who d. London 1860. Issue : one son
Augustus, b. 1825 ?
ii William, b. Middle row, Truro, 3 Aug. 1791,
held an appointment in the War Office in 1813.
Sailed from Penzance to Leghorn where he d. of
consumption, 1 Mch. 1826, bur. the Cemetery.
iii Charles, b. Middle row, Truro, 8 Sep. 1793,
Clerk in H.M. Customs, Truro, Dec. 1815, to Feb.
1828, Searcher Feb. 1828 to Mch. 1837, Controller
at Bridport, Mch. 1837 to June 1841 Collector
at Gweek June 1841 to Apl. 1846, Controller
at Lancaster Apl. 1846 to Oct. 1846, Controller
at Falmouth Oct. 1846 to May 1848, Collector
at New Ross, Wexford May 1848 to Sep,
1853, Collector at Lancaster Sep. 1853 to Jan.
1854, Controller at Exeter Jan. 1854 to Aug.
1860, when he retired on his full salary. d.
Alverton, Penzance, 29 Nov. 1870, bur. the Cemetery, where is Tombstone, m. (1) St. Clement's
7 Sep. 1826, Sarah dau. of Benjamin and Ann
Barwis. She was b. 10 Jan. 1797, and d. Truro
Vean, Truro, 28 Feb. 1833, and bur. Kenwyn, 4
Mch. C. Sholl m. (2) 1 Feb. 1840, Sarah dau. of
Rev. Robert Broadley, R. of Bridport, Dorset, by
Ann his wife. Sarah Broadley was b. Caltistock,
Dorset, 16 June 1811, and still survives. The issue
of the first marriage were: a Charles William ; b
Robert Horatio ; c Ellen Mary and d Sarah Anne.
a Charles William, b. Truro Vean, 1 Nov. 1827.
Educated at the Mining school, Tuckingmill,
and at Bellevue; articled pupil to Mr. George
Wightwick, architect, Plymouth; resident in
U.S. of America 185 - to 1864. Patentee in
" Improvements in compressed air hammers."
b Robert Horatio b. Truro Vean 16 April 1829,
held a situation in the Truro Bank, d. of con-
sumption at Treath, Helford 8 July 1845, bur.
Manaccan, where is monument.
c Ellen Mary b. Truro Vean, 26 Sep. 1831, bap. St.
Mary's 21 Oct., m. St. Leonards, Exeter 25 Oct.
1859, George eldest son of Henry Hirtzel, Official
Assignee, Bankruptcy Court, Exeter. Mr. G.
Hirtzel, b. 30 Dec. 1832, is a solicitor in practice
at Exeter. The issue of this m. are (1) Sophia
Mary b. Exeter 28 November 1860 ; (2) Ellen
Sarah b. Exeter 13 May 1862 ; (3) George
Clement b. Exeter 11 Sep. 1864 ; (4) Charles
Henry b. Exeter 10 Aug. 1865; (5) Arthur
Francis b. 6 Oct. 1867 ; (6) Beatrice Caroline b.
23 January 1869 ; (7) Henry Melchior b. 24
May 1870 ; (8) Barnard Turner b. 2 Sep. 1871 ;
(9) Guy Dashwood b. 6 Nov. 1872.
d Sarah Anne b. Truro Vean 23 Feb. 1833, d.
Mount Radford, Exeter 8 Sep. 1857, bur. St.
Leonard's, where is a monument.
iv Robert b. Rosewin row, Truro 4 Nov. 1797.
An Officer in the surveying voyages of H. M.
Ships " Adventurer and Beagle." Mate of the
"Adventurer" 1826, Lieut. Beagle 1826. Lieut.
of the " Beagle" 1826, d. at sea on board the
"Beagle" 20 Jan. 1827, bur. Port San Julian,
Patagonia, where is monu.
v Jonah b. Rosewin row, Truro, 25 Nov. 1800, d. of
cholera at Quebec, Sep. 1834.

i Jemima Mary b. Middle row, Truro, 2 Apl. 1793
d. South Parade, Bath, 3 Feb. 1870, bur. in Miss
Mary Smith's vault in Widcombe Cemetery She
m. at Bridport 5 Sep. 1839 George Stallard,
Solicitor, who d. 3 Laura place, Bath, 10 Nov.
1847 aged 57, and was bur. in Bath Easton churchyard. Mr. Stallard by a previous mar. had five
children, (1) George, V. of East Grafton, who m.
Miss Taylor, and has issue Arthur Gordon, Curate
of Cardiff, m. Ellen Brown, and Florence who m.
Rev. Charles Edward Hammond, formerly Fellow
of Exeter Coll. Oxf., and has issue, (2) Edward, a
Solicitor ; and three daughters, Eliza, Caroline
and Annie.
ii Charlotte, *see* Bonse, J. J. A. ante col. 11.
2 Richard b. 14 Jan., bap. 17 Feb. 1771, d. Gloucester
17 Mch. 1796, monu. there.
3 William b. 6 Oct., bapt. 7 Nov. 1773, d. 15 Oct.
bur. 17 Oct. 1790.
4 Martin b. 11 June 1777, bapt. 10 July 1778, held a
situation in a Solicitor's office, d. London. He m.
Jane dau. of Peter Floyd of Truro, and their children
were
i John bapt. St. Mary's, Truro, 24 Oct. 1794.
ii Betsey bapt. St. Mary's, 25 Feb. 1798.
iii Catherine bur. St. Mary's, 15 Sep. 1802.
iv Cecilia bapt. St. Mary's, 3 Feb. 1803.
v Jane Floyd bapt. St. Mary's, 16 Feb. 1805.
vi Emma bapt. St. Mary's, 7 Apl. 1807, bur. St. Mary
14 May.
vii James bapt. St. Mary's, 1 Apl. 1808, bur. St.
Mary's 15 Oct. 1809.
Two other children, Martin and Richard, emigrated
to Perth, Western Australia.
5 John bapt. 6 Jan. 1783, bur. 4 Nov. 1784.
1 Mary b. 13 Dec. 1767, d. 4 Feb., bur. 6 Feb. 1768.
2 Mary b. 14 Jan. and privately bapt. 5 Feb. 1769,
m. 7 Dec. 1801, John Mathews of Kenwyn.
3 Elizabeth b. 24 Oct. and bapt. 23 Nov. 1775, bur.
25 July 1777.
4 Elizabeth b. 17 Mch. and bapt. 21 May 1780, ? m.
26 May 1811 Henry Hill.
(1) Mary Sholl, only dau. of Richard Sholl,wh. d. 1745,
was bap. 27 Jan. 1731, m. John Tregelles of St. Agnes.

There were other Sholls in Kenwyn, closely related to the
above, but we cannot trace the relationship clearly at
present.
(1) William, bur. 29 May 1711, m. 3 Ap. 1666 (? Jane)
Roberts, bur. 5 Dec. 1708, and had by her Mary, bap.
20 Oct. 1668, and another dau. b. 1675.
(2) Robert, m. Mary Lauyon 25 Dec. 1721; a Robert was
bur. 13 Oct. 1765.
(3) Richard (perhaps the father of Richard of Bosvigo),
bur. 5 Ap. 1731, m. and had Margaret, bap. 8. Jan.
1700; Jane, bap. 5 Aug. 1702, bur. 15 Aug. 1707; Amy,
bap. 1 Nov. 1704 ; Mary, bap. 1 Nov. 1706; Jane, bap.
6 Oct. 1711.
(4) William, bur. 12 Dec. 1754, m. (? Amy, bur. 27 Jan.
1746), and had Nicholas, William, Margaret, Elizabeth,
Margaret, Amy, Jane, Margery.
1 Nicholas, bap. 7 Oct. 1735, bur. 30 Mch. 1737.
2 William (?twin), bap. 7 Oct. 1735, bur 23 Dec.
1772, m. 10 Dec. 1759, Mary James of Kenwyn,
and had by her William, Nicholas, Abraham, Richard,
Catherine, Elizabeth.
i William, bap. 6 Mch. 1761, ? bur. 8 Feb. 1779.
ii Nicholas, bap. 1 May 1768.
iii Abraham, bap. 11 Jan. 1771, privately ; he witn.
11 Feb. 1836, m. of William Sholl with Maria
Roberts of Kenwyn.
iv Richard, bap. 6 June 1773, " son of William

deceased," bur. 1 Mch. 1775, "son of Mary widow."

i Catherine, bap. 1 Sep. 1760.

ii Elizabeth, bap. 6 Oct. 1765, bur. 24 May 1771.

1 Margaret, bur. 22 Aug. 1730.

2 Elizabeth, bap. 13 June 1730.

3 Margaret. bap. 6 Ap. 1733, m. 27 Dec. 1755 Antony Dale of Kenwyn (witn. William Sholl).

4 Amy, bap. 17 Mch. 173⅝, ? bur. 27 Jan. 171⅞.

5 Jane, bap. 5 Oct. 1740, bur. 27 Dec. 1746.

6 Margery, bap. 10 June 1744.

(5) Robert (? 4 son of Richard of Bosvigo), m. Jane (? Nicholls) and had by her John, ? bap. 20 July 1802, bur. 10 Sep. 1802; John Nicholls, bap. 28 July 1805; Grace Nicholls, bap. 6 Mch. 1808, bur. 10 Oct. 1811; William, bap. 10 Sep. 1815, ? m. 11 Feb. 1836, Maria Roberts of Kenwyn (witn. Abraham Sholl).

(6) John Henry, son of Henry and Sarah Sholl, Castle st., bap. 9 July 1837.

(7) (? Henry) child of R. Sholl, bap. 6 Jan. 172⅞.

There were also Sholls in Madron : a dau. of Ralph Shoale was bur. there 30 June 1663 : Elizabeth Sholl m. 13 July 1761, Nicholas Blake, both of Penzance (witn. Thomas Bradley, Nehemiah Batten) ; Margery Sholl of Penzance, m. 7 Aug. 1769, Philip Johns of St. Ives. Amy Sholl m. † 3 Nov. 1733, Thomas Harry, both of Penzance : he was bap. 2 Feb. 170⅔ son of Robert Harry, junr., who m. † 1 Apl. 1700 Mary Prouse of Madron. Thomas Sholl of Madron bur. † 8 May 1707. Jane m. † 12 Jan. 1749 John Matthew both of Penzance.

At Paul, Jane dau. of Thomas Sholl was bap. 10 Nov. 1683 ; Thomas the father was bur. 19 Fch. 168⅚.

The name occurs also at Padstow and at St. Minver (Sir J. Maclean's History of Trigg Minor, i, 528 ; ii, 172 : iii, 33.

A son of Abraham Sholl, late of Camborne, was born 21 Oct. 1869, Talbot road, Clunes, Victoria, Australia.

SYMES.

JOHN, son of Edward and Sophia Symes of Bridgewater, was b. Bridgewater 19 July 1810. He was minister in charge of the Apostolic church at Paddington, and afterwards of that at Southwark. For some years previous to this he had resided in Jersey. After a life of ministerial activity, he became suddenly ill after the exertion of the Christmas services, and went to Hastings for a rest, became worse, and after ten days of suffering, during which he was either insensible or raving, he d. there 15 Jan. 1873, bur. Kensal Green. He m. St. Stephen's, Bristol, 16 May 1837 Rosanna seventh dau. of Henry Boase by Anne Craige. She was b. Penzance 23 Jan. 1814, and privately bapt. by Rev. C. V. Le Grice, d. suddenly early in the morning of Thursday 26 June 1856 in Mr. John Belcher's house, bur. Kensal Green. Their children were

(1) Edward Henry b. St. Hellier's, Jersey, 8 June 1838, d. Paddington 24 July 1843, bur. Paddington churchyard.

(2) John Anstice b. Paddington 12 Oct. 1845, d. Thursday 26 June 1851.

(3) Peter Barclay b. Paddington 16 (or 23) Sep. 1847, educated as a Civil Engineer at King's Coll. London. Went to Canada and obtained employment in a Government office in Ottawa, came home to see his parents in 1872, and after the death of his father left Liverpool for Canada 17 Apl. 1873 accompanied by his sister Ellen, and is now engaged in the Dominion Surveying Department.

(4) Alfred b. Southwark 5 July 1849, d. an infant.

E

(1) Ellen Colmer b. St. Hellier's 18 Sep. 1840, bapt. C. A. Church. Now in Canada.

(2) Jessie Barclay b. St. Hollier's 16 May 1842, d. Paddington 12 Oct. 1844, bur. Paddington churchyard.

(3) Emily Rosa b. St. Hellier's 21 Sep. 1843, d. St. Hellier's an infant.

Mr. John Symes m. (2) his cousin Annie, dau. of Mr. Warren, who still survives.

THOMSON OF PLYMOUTH.

ARTHUR THOMSON was b. 27 Feb. 1738, and m. 7 Sep. 1764 Agnes Kay. She was b. 21 Mch. 1740. The issue were (1) Agnes b. 17 Jan. 1765 ; (2) Arthur, of whom presently ; (3) Jane b. Apl. 1770 : (4) William b. 19 Apl. 1772; (5) Mary b. 22 Apl. 1774 ; (6) David b. 15 Apl. 1776 ; (7) Anne b. 18 Sep. 1778 ; (8) Margaret b. 2 Nov. 1781.

Arthur Thomson of Lasswade near Edinburgh was b. 20 Jan. 1768, d. 21 Nov. 1848, m. (1) 22 Jan. 1794 Margaret Mitchel, b. 6 Apl. 1773, d. in giving birth to her sixth child Mitchel 22 Sep. 1804. The issue of this marriage were (1) Catherine b. 20 Dec. 1794 ; (2) Agnes b. 21 May 1796 ; (3) Minnie b. 8 Sep. 1798 ; (4) Jane b. 19 Feb. 1800 (5) Mary b. 25 Jan. 1802 ; (6) Mitchel, of whom below.

Arthur Thomson m. (2) 13 Jan. 1805 his cousin Agnes McClaren, she d. 2 May 1862 leaving no issue.

Mitchel Thomson, Fleet Surgeon R.N., was b. Lasswade 22 Sep. 1804, and educated at the parish school there and at Edinburgh. On 20 May 1819 he entered on his apprenticeship in medicine with Dr. Renton at Pennycuick, went to Edinburgh University 1 Nov. 1822, apprenticeship expired 20 May 1823, went as assistant to Dr. Renton, junr., Peebles, 1 Apr. 1824, passed the College of Surgeons, London, 2 Dec. 1825, passed the Navy Board 13 Dec. 1825, joined Haslar Hospital as assistant surgeon the following day. The 3 June 1826 was appointed to the "Surly," cruising in the North Sea, to the "Britannia" flagship at Portsmouth 1 Aug. 1828, to the "Barham" flagship, West Indies, 5 Aug. 1828, ordered to wait for a passage out in H.M.S. "Victory," but did not take up the appointment. To the "Asia," Sir Pultney Malcolm's flagship, in the Mediterranean 3rd Oct. 1828. Went out in the "Madagascar," and was appointed senior assistant surgeon to the "Revenge," Capt. Norman Thomson, lying at Naples, ordered to take a passage in the "Hind," Captain Rob. January 1 went to Malta Hospital sick. January 17 1830 sent home in the "Neva," transport ship, Captain Adamson, in charge of sick. Oct. 31 1830 passed the Royal College of Surgeons, Edinburgh. Nov. 2 1830 passed the Navy Board as surgeon. 26 Nov. 1830 appointed supernumerary assistant to the "Vincent" at Portsmouth. 1831 Feb. 16 appointed to the "Maidstone," flagship of Commodore Schomberg, Cape of Good Hope, took passage in the "Ceres" as far as the Mauritius, then in the "Talbot," Captain Dickenson. Oct. 30 1831 he was appointed assistant surgeon to the Royal Naval Hospital, Cape of Good Hope. 1832 surgeon of the flagship "Undaunted," Captain Harvey. Jan. 31 1833 invalided to England, sailed in the merchant ship "Spartan." 7 Jan. 1834 appointed to the "Eclipse." 18 Feb. 1834 sent to the Royal Naval Hospital, Plymouth, in consequence of an injury from a fall, March 5 1834 appointed to H.M.S. "Pandora." Married 8 Oct. 1835 at Budock Church, Falmouth, paid a short visit to Paris, and then was in practice a short time in Bristol, where he had not the pleasure of a single patient. April 1837 appointed to H.M.S. "Sappho" in the West Indies. 1839 published a letter in the Falmouth packet "On the importance of sending educated black missionaries to Africa." The same year published "An address to the blacks on mission work." 1842 commenced practice in Penzance. Health failed, and in 1845 came to Plymouth and commenced practice. June 1 1847 appointed to H.M.S. "Odin," Captain the Honble. F. Pelham. 20 Oct. 1849 he brought out his signal night lights for ships, printed his first book at Malta. 1851 printed his second book on night signal lights. 1852 sent a proposition and plan after a meeting with Lieut. Lambert of H.M.S. "Odin" to Sir Edward Parry for united action in H.M. service for prayer. Out of this originated the Royal Naval Scripture Readers' Society, which now employs fourteen readers, and has an income of £2,000 a-year. This year he published his third book on night signals under the authority of and paid for by the Admiralty. Was ordered to sea by the Admiralty and worked them with success for five months. 1853 invented a slush lamp for decks, ordered by the Admiralty to test the plans on board the flagship "Royal Adelaide" at Plymouth. Offered to light all ships with his slush lamps. All ships in H.M. service are now lighted on his plans. Printed and published "Night signals for merchant ships." Appointed to the "Russell" coastguard ship at Falmouth in 1854, then to the "Royal William," taking in her 1,100 French troops to the Baltic during the Russian war. Was present at the attack on Bomarsund. Brought home 700 Russian prisoners, of these 200 fell ill with cholera, twenty five died; none of the crew however suffered. He received the war medal. In 1856 he once more commenced to practice at Plymouth, being put on half-pay, and so continued for four years. During 1860 he was appointed to the "Royal Adelaide," then to the "Wellington," and then to the "Impregnable" training ship for boys at Devonport. An attack of inflammation of the lungs in 1862, being thirty-six years after his first entering the navy, incapacitated him for further service afloat, and he took his retirement. In 1863 he received the Greenwich Hospital pension. He is the author of "Tabular instruction for schools," and "Tabular chronology," and "Tabular chronology for England, Scotland, &c. without the use of figures," "Tabular teaching of Scriptures for schools and families," etc. Was president of the Penzance Institute Oct. 1845, and on leaving the town received a present of a silver inkstand. In 1860 he was surgeon to the "Pride of Devon" lodge of Odd Fellows ; whilst practising in Plymouth on being appointed to a ship he resigned and received a testimonial of a piece of plate. The following are the titles of some of his works:— " System of general night signals for the use of H.M. ships and squadrons," G. Muir, Malta, 1850, 2s. ; second edition of same. F. Nicholson. Plymouth, 1852 ; third edition,1852 ; " Code of night signals on a system wherein colored lights are introduced, arranged for the use of Her Majesty's navy by order of the Lord Commissioners of the Admiralty August, 1853."

His wife Grace Lucilla, sixth dau. of Hon. Bonse and Anne Craige, was b. 127, Sloane street, Chelsea, 27 Mch. 1809, and privately bapt. by the Rev. John Townshend. She came to Penzance with her parents in 1811. In 1833 she went to Falmouth, and resided with her sister Laura Elizabeth Boase until 8 Oct. 1835, when she was m. at Budock church by the Rev. Geo. Kempe to Mitchel Thomson, surgeon R.N. as before mentioned. The issue of this marriage were (1) Arthur Henry, (2) Lewis Charles, (3) Alfred Mitchell, (4) Eustace Boase, (5) Lionel, (6) Sidney Lambert, (1) Jessie Anna, (2) Lucy Emily.

(1) Arthur Henry Thomson was b. Queen square, Bristol, 5 Jan. 1837, and bapt. at Bridge street Chapel by the Rev. Henry Roper. He went to Penzance with his parents in 1837, and in Oct. 1845 removed to Plymouth, his education was received at the Plymouth Grammar School under Mr. Bennett, head roaster, and at Mr. Weymouth's Portland Grammar School. Leaving school at the age of fifteen he entered as a clerk in the accountant's office of the South Devon Railway. On the 8 Dec. 1855 he was appointed to a clerkship in

H.M. Dockyard, Devonport, here he gradually rose until he had become Store Keeper at Keyham, and had good prospects of further advancement; ill health however obliged him to quit the service, and he retired on a pension 8 Dec. 1873. He m. 11 June 1867 Caroline, b. 23 Jan. 1837, dau. of Henry and Emma Steele, and has by her i Archibald Steele b. 20 June 1868 ; ii Arthur Leonard b. 6 Aug. 1869; i Fanny Steele b. 13 Oct. 1870: ii Jessie Boase b. 25 Mch. 1872 ; iii Emma Caroline b. 16 Feb. 1874.

(2) Lewis Charles Thomson was b. 26, Clarence street, Penzance 17 July 1843, and bap. at the Independent Chapel by the Rev. John Foxell. About two years after his birth his parents removed to Frankfort street, Plymouth. He was educated at Dr. Weymouth's Portland Grammar School, Portland Villas, Plymouth, from 1853 to 1858, and then entered the Accountant's Office of the South Devon Railway, where he remained from Christmas 1858 to 15 Feb. 1861. He removed to London after this and became a clerk in the office of the well known Parliamentary shorthand writers, Messrs. W. B. Gurney and Sons, 26, Abingdon Street, Westminster. The work here during the parliamentary session, Feb.—Aug. 1861, was so hard and the confinement so bad for the health, that, although the remuneration was considerable, he was obliged to resign his situation. On the 26 May 1862 after passing a competitive examination he got an appointment of a clerkship under the Admiralty at H.M. Dockyard, Portsmouth, where he remained until 18 Sep. 1864, when he was removed to H.M. Dockyard, Devonport, where he still remains. He married at St. Mary's, Penzance 3 Jan. 1874 his first cousin Julia second dau. of J. J. A. Boase, who was b. at Lariggan, near Penzance 5 Mch. 1840, and bap. by the Rev. Edward Shuttleworth, at St. Mary's, Penzance, 10 Apl. She passed first class in the theory of music under the scheme of the Society for the Encouragement of Arts and Manufactures in London Apl. 1871, and received a certificate dated 28 June 1871. During 1872 and 1873 she nursed her mother with the greatest care and kindness, and continued her attention to her until her decease 10 Sep. 1873. She m. Lewis Charles Thomson, as before mentioned : the issue of this marriage is a son Charles Bertram b. 14, Seaton Terrace, Mutley, Plymouth 19 May 1873, bap. St. Andrew's, Plymouth 28 July.

(3) Alfred Mitchell Thomson was b. 26 Clarence street, Penzance, 10 Apl. 1845, and bapt. at the Independent Chapel by the Rev. John Foxell: came with his parents to Plymouth in 1845, and was educated at Mr. Greave's, Mr. Weymouth's, and the Rev. Dr. Holmes' Schools. In Oct. 1863, at eighteen years of age, he went with his brother Eustace to the University of Glasgow to study medicine, and took his M.B. and M.Ch. degrees in 1869. He then acted as Assistant to Mr. Alfred Prideaux, Liskeard ; to Mr. John C. Duke, Lewisham road, Greenwich; and to Mr. George P. Goldsmith, Bedford. After that he went as Surgeon in the "Ottawa" Allan's Line of Steamers to the United States and Canada, and remained in that Company's service ten months, when he left and joined the Royal Mail Steam Packet Co., and was appointed to the " Mersey " trading between the West India Islands. He was, however, lost overboard off Demerara, 27 Nov. 1872, during the night, and his remains were not recovered.

(4) Eustace Boase Thomson was b. 14, Frankfort street, Plymouth, 6 Apl. 1846, and bapt. at Norley Independent Chapel by the Rev. Ebenezer Jones. After being educated at Dr. Weymouth's and the Rev. Dr. Holmes' Schools, at the age of seventeen, in Oct. 1863 he went with his brother Alfred to the University of Glasgow

to study medicine, took his M.B. and M.Ch. degrees in
May 1867, and then went as an Assistant to Henry
Barber, M.D., Ulverstone, Lancashire, for twelve
months. He then acted as locum tenens for Amos
Beardsley, M.R.C.S., Grange-over-sands, Lancashire,
then as locum tenens for Augustus Johnston, M.B.,
Hawkshead, Lancashire, for six weeks ; then as Assistant to Daniel Wheeler, M.R.C.S., Chelmsford, for
twenty months ; then as locum tenens for Henry Clothier,
M.R.C.S., Haslemere, Surrey, then as as locum tenens for
Mr. Muriel, Whitehaven, for three months His next
appointment was that of House Surgeon at the Essex
and Colchester Hospital, Colchester, where he remained
two years and a half. He took his M.D. degree in
Glasgow 1872, and was registered in England on the
21 July of the same year. In Nov. 1873 he returned
to his native town, and commenced practice as a
physician and surgeon.
(5) Lionel Thomson b. 4 Oxford street, Plymouth, 19
Feb. 1851, d. of scarlet fever Plymouth 26 Feb.
(6) Sidney Lambert Thomson b. 4 Oxford street, Plymouth, 21 Mch. 1852, d. of convulsions from teething,
Plymouth 20 Apl. 1853.
(1) Jessie Anna Thomson b. Penzance 16 May 1842, d.
of croup, Penzance 16 Oct. 1845, bur. St Mary's churchyard in her grandfather's vault.
(2) Lucy Emily Thomson b. 4 Oxford street, Plymouth,
19 Sep. 1849, and privately bapt. by the Rev. E. Steer
of Batter street Chapel.

TONKIN AND BODINNAR OF PAUL.

PAUL TONKIN of Newlyn, m. Elizabeth and had by her
Joseph b. 10 Oct. 1762, d. 22 Jan. 1836, m. Paul 10 Dec.
1792, Jane dau. of Arthur Bouse and Jane Lugg. She was
b. Madron 1 Jan. 1766 and bapt. 25 Jan., d. Newlyn, 6
Feb. 1856. The issue were
(1) Henry Bouse b. Newlyn 11 Feb. 1795. Was educated
at the expense of his uncle Mr. Henry Bouse, with the
intention of his taking a place in the Penzance Union
Bank, but being determined to go to sea, he bound
himself apprentice to Capt. Rosewall, master of a
Penzance trader. For some time he himself commanded
a merchantman, but eventually he settled at Hobart
Town, Tasmania, and acted as one of Lloyds' Surveyors
and Chairman of the Marine Board. He m. 1822 at
St. Saviour's, Southwark, Elizabeth Saunders of Southwark, but has no issue. One of Elizabeth Saunders'
sisters is married to George Wilson, merchant, Hobart
Town.
(1) Harriet b. 24 Oct. 1793, d. an infant.
(2) Caroline Naomi b. 12 Dec. 1801, d. Newlyn 2 Jan.
1870, m. Paul 1 Apl. 1826, Stephen Bodinnar of
Newlyn, b. 12 May 1801. Their children are i Jane
Mary, ii Harriet, iii Christopher Henry, iv Caroline
Naomi, v Joseph Tonkin, vi Ellen.
i Jane Mary b. 5 Jan. 1828, m. 4 Apl. 1851, Nicholas
Harvey of Newlyn, and had by him I Stephen, b.
1853 ; II Nicholas b. 1855 ; III Ellen b. 1857 ;
IV Harriet b. 1860, d. Newlyn Aug. 1875 ; V Jane
b. 1862 ; VI Caroline b. 1870.
ii Harriet b. 19 Apl. 1830, d. 7 July 1858, m. May
1855 Richard Tonkin, who. d. 1869. Issue Joseph
b. 1856.
iii Christopher Henry b. 9 Nov. 1831, d. 1 May 1856
unm.
iv Caroline Naomi b. 7 Feb. 1836, m. 1857 William
Hocking, farmer, Kelynack, St. Just, and has by him
I William b. 1859 ; II Christopher b. 1861 ; III
James b. 1863 ; IV Joseph b. 1865 ; V John b. 1867 ;

E²

VI Benjamin b. 1869 ; VII Nicholas b. 1871 ; VIII
Anne b. 1874, and two others who d. in infancy.
v Joseph Tonkin b. 17 Aug. 1839, m. Madron 8 Oct.
1871 Charlotte youngest dau. of Jacob Corin of
Higher Boskenning, Madron, and has by her Lydia
b. 1872 and Henry Tonkin b. 1875.
vi Ellen b. 6 May 1841, d. 15 Aug. 1841.

TREWAVAS OF PAUL.

A JOHN TREWAVAS of Mousehole, bur. 28 Jan. 1778, m. *
15 Ap. 1710 Charity eld. dau. of Arthur Bouse, bur. * 17
March 1777, and had by her
(1) Joan bap. * 16 Feb. 1711⁹.
(2) Margaret bap. * 22 March 171⁴⁵, d. before 1721.
(3) John of Mousehole bap. * 25 Ap. 1719, bur. 5 Ap.
1779, widower.
(4) Margaret bap. * 11 July 1721, living 1779, m. † 18
Feb. 1753 Stephen Luke.
(5) William junior bap. * 30 Jan. 172³⁴, bur. 26 May 1805,
age 82. m. * 18 Sep. 1748 Ann dau. of (? Bernard)
Yearnat, bur. 24 Jan. 174⁴⁸, and had issue
1 Joan bap. * 5 Feb. 174⁹⁵.
2 John bap. * 4 Nov. 1750.
3 Anne bap. * 1 Oct. 1752.
4 Jane bap. * 12 June 1754.
5 Ruth bap. * 7 Dec. 1755.
6 John bap. * 30 Nov. 1757.
7 William bap. * 2 Jan. 1760.
8 Richard bap. * 2 Jan. 1760.
9 Sarah bap. * 8 Nov. 1761.
10 William bap. * 19 Oct. 1766.
(6) Elizabeth bap. * 10 Oct. 1726.

B William Trewavas of Mousehole m. * 28 March 1749
Mary dau. of (? Bernard) Yeaman, bur. * 30 March 1723,
bur. * 30 May 1802, age 78, ' married,' and had by her
(1) Mary bap. * 6 March 175⁹.
(2) Elizabeth bap. * 23 July 1753.
(3) Jane bap. * 14 Feb. 1755.
(4) John bap. * 28 Oct. 1758.

C A daughter of Trewavas m. Thomas Rogers of Lanke
circa 1380.

TWEEDY.

MR. TWEEDY m. Mary Atkins who was b. 27 Aug. 1646,
and d. 30 Sep. 1708. Their son James b. 1682, d. 1 Sep.
1737, m. 31 Jan. 170⁹ Elizabeth (Surthin ?) who d. 3 May
1720. Up to this period the name was generally spelt
Twedy. James Tweedy's issue were 1 William ; 2 Joseph
Surthin b. 13 July 1715 ; 3 Timothy b. 8 Dec. 1716.
William Tweedy b. 18 Nov. 1708. d. 23 May 1780, m. 18
May 1765, Margaret Bainbridge ; their son William b. 18
July 1766, came from London to Truro in connection with
the Messrs. Praed's Bank, and was the first of his family
who settled in Cornwall. He d. Truro 21 Mch. 1854, m. 6
Feb. 1796 Anne dau. of Will. Naudin. She d. Truro Vean 24
Jan. 1867, aged 94. Their children were (1) William Mansell; (2) John; (3) Charles; (4) Robert; (5) Alfred; (6) Henry;
(7) John William; (8) Edward Brian. (1) Mary ; (2) Margaret : (3) Elizabeth ; (4) Philippa ; (5) Caroline.
(1) William Mansell b 6 Dec. 1796, Banker Truro, Chairman of the Cornwall Railway Co., Secretary of the
Royal Institution of Cornwall 1818-56, and President
1857-59, Treasurer of the Royal Horticultural Society
of Cornwall, the Royal Cornwall Infirmary, the Bible
Society, and the Church Missionary Society. One of

the chief promoters of the Truro Training College, d. Alverton, Truro 17 Apl. 1859, memorial window in Kenwyn Church, m. 28 Jan. 1826 at Newcastle? his cousin Jane Tanner, but left no issue.

(2) John b. 8 Feb. 1708, d. 9 Aug. 1708.

(3) Charles b. 19 May 1799, held a situation in the Cornish Bank, d. Truro Vean of rapid consumption 18 Apl. 1822.

(4) Robert, of whom presently.

(5) Alfred b. July 1808, d. 6 Sep. 1808.

(6) Henry, b. 4 Mch. 1811, d. 4 May 1811.

(7) John Williams, b. 12 Feb. 1813, d. Truro Vean, 23 Oct. 1822.

(8) Edward Brian, Banker, Falmouth, b. 4 Aug. 1814, d. suddenly at Homburg, 13 July 1869, m. Elizabeth Paul Rogers, dau of Mr. Rogers, Solicitor, Helston. No issue.

(1) Mary, b. 22 Nov. 1800, m. Falmouth, 13 Oct. 1825, Joseph Talwin Foster, b. Bromley, Middlesex, d. Stamford hill, 2 Feb. 1861.

(2) Margaret Anne, b. 16 July 1802, d. Truro Vean, 19 Apl. 1820.

(3) Elizabeth, b. 12 Nov. 1804.

(4) Phillipa, b. 28 May 1807, d. 10 Oct. 1807.

(5) Caroline, b. 31 August. 1809.

Robert Tweedy b. 13 Mch. 1806, Banker, Redruth, then at Truro, Chairman of the Cornwall Railway, m. Kea, 26 July 1831, Harriet second dau. of Samuel Milford by Ann Jenkins, b. 22 Nov. 1806. Their children are (1) William, (2) Robert Milford, (3) John William, (4) Charles, (5) Henry John, (6) Alfred Edward, (7) Frederick Williams, (1) Ann, (2) Harriet Mary, (3) Philippa, (4) Elizabeth Jane.

(1) William b. Rosewyn row, Truro, 30 May 1832, Banker, Truro, m. 1868, Mary Dobbs. Issue, a dau. b. 3 Nov. 1871, d. an infant, William Mansel, b. 19 Dec. 1873, d. Brick House, Truro, 23 Jan. 1874.

(2) Robert Milford b. Redruth, 30 Nov 1834. Formerly manager of the Cornish Bank, Redruth, became manager of the Cornish Bank, Falmouth, 1862, m. St. Mary's. Penzance, 22 July 1863 his second cousin Charlotte Anne, eldest dau. of J. J. A. Boase and Charlotte Sholl, b. 30 Jan. 1833. Their children are Edith Annie, b. Falmouth, 7 May 1864, bapt. 1 June; Arthur Clement, b. Falmouth, 31 July 1866, bapt. 29 Aug.

(3) John William b. Redruth 4 Oct. 1836, d. Redruth 23 May 1837.

(4) Charles b. Redruth 19 May 1841, manager of the Cornish Bank Redruth, 1862, m. St. Just in Roseland, 24 May 1866, Edith Sophia, second dau. of Rev. C. Winstanley Carlyon, R. of St. Just in Roseland. Their children are Charles Winstanley b. Redruth 7 Mch. 1867; Reginald Carlyon b. Redruth 11 Dec. 1868; Robert Naudin b. Redruth 18 Meh. 1875: Edith Mabel b. Redruth 21 Nov. 1870; Alice Harriet b. The Elms, Redruth 9 Nov. 1872: d. The Elms 6 Feb. 1874.

(5) Henry John b. Redruth 23 June 1843, educated at Hitchin Free School, matriculated at the University of London, 1860, B.A. Nov. 1862, called to the Bar at Lincoln's Inn 5 June 1868, Draughtsman and Conveyancer at 5 Old square, Lincoln's Inn, m. Kenwyn 7 Apl. 1874, Maria Louisa second dau. of Edward Trewbody Carlyon, Solicitor. b. Truro, 19 Apl. 1846. Issue,

Dorothea b. 151 Cornwall road, Notting-hill, 30 Dec. 1874.

(6) Alfred Edward b. Redruth 10 Nov. 1846. In a Tea Broker's office in London, but falling into a consumption, went a voyage to Australia, returned to England and d. Tregolls, Truro 25 Jan. 1874, bur. Kenwyn.

(7) Frederick Williams b. 26 Oct. 1848, d. 28 Feb. 1849.

(1) Ann b. Rosewin row, Truro 19 July 1833, d. Redruth 28 July 1846.

(2) Harriet Mary b. Redruth 30 Jan. 1838.

(3) Philippa b. Redruth 24 May 1839, m. Kenwyn 6 June 1867, William youngest son of Henry Ashworth of the Oaks, Bolton le Moor.

(4) Elizabeth Jane b. Redruth 3 May 1845.

Robert Tweedy with his three sons William, Robert Milford, and Charles in connection with Sir Frederick Martin Williams of Tregullow, M.P. for Truro, constitute the firm of Messrs. Tweedy, Williams, and Co., Bankers at Truro, Redruth, Falmouth, and Penryn.

Philippa Naudin, sister of Mrs. William Tweedy, was b. at Hackney, it is believed, 17 Feb. 1774, she d. Burncoose Gwennap 7 Dec. 1861, m. the Friends' Meeting House, Perranarworthal 27 June 1810 John son of John Williams and Catherine dau. of Martin Harvey of Killefreth, b. Gwennap, 3 Aug. 1777, d. Burncoose 11 Aug. 1849, bur. the Friends' ground, Redruth, where his wife also lies. See Sir J. Maclean's "History of Trigg Minor," ii, 435, 442.

WALLIS OF MADRON AND BODMIN.

NICHOLAS WALLIS of Madron m. Ann eld. dau. of Thomas Hosking of Landithy in Madron, and had by her

(1) Christopher, solicitor of Helston, bought Trevarno in Sithney, d. 4 Dec. 1826, aged 82, m. Philippa dau. of Roberts of Helston, d. 22 July 1807, aged 67; and had by her an heiress Philippa, d. 18 Feb. 1859, aged 84, m. Capt. Joseph Lamb Popham, R.N., who d. 22 Feb. 1833, aged 62.

(2) Nicholas.

(3) Thomas, collector of Customs at St. Ives.

(4) John, solicitor, b. † 1759, d. Bodmin 2 Ap. 1842, moved from Helston to Bodmin 1 Jan 1794, m. Isabella Mary dau of Henry Sloggett by Isabella Mary sister and coheiress of John Samuel Silly, and had by her

1 John b. Bodmin 11 Ap. 1789, d. 6 Dec. 1866, bur. 11 Dec., at Exeter College 7 Dec. 1813, B.A. 7 July 1820, M.A. 20 Mch. 1821, Vicar of Bodmin 17 Nov. 1817 to 1866. Official of the Archdeacon of Cornwall 1840, and resident for some years at St. Gluvias. Author of "The Bodmin Register" and other works.

1 Ann Julia d. Bodmin 4 Aug. 1871, aged 80.

2 Louisa m. Bodmin 1832 Rev. William Morshead, b. 1805.

(5) Elizabeth m. Bullock.

(6) Ann m. † 26 Ap. 1771 William Penrose of Penzance, witness Mary Penrose.

(7) Mary.

(8) Jane m. Thomas Leggoe.

Robert Wallis had a seat in Penzance Church 1674.

MANOR OF ALVERTON.

RICHARD DANIELL'S Annual High Rents 1654 and Conventionary Rents 1657.—

High Rents 1654.

	£	s.	d.
Bosasian, St. Just, Rich. Angwin	1	8	
„ „ Jo. Angwin	2	0	
Trigovara, Rich. Ludnow	1	0	
Thomas Holla	1	2	
Custom House and Champion, H. Polkinhorne (part of arrears)	3	0	
Trowronock, Rob. Baynard ..	4	2	
Tenures in Penzance, Rich. Trewen.. ..	3	6	
Treruf in Sennen, Rich. Treruf ..	2	0	
Trembath, Jo. Ellis (part of arrears) ..	5	0	
Bodenar Wartha in Sancreed, W. Hand ..	2	2	
Auhra 5s, Lamarna 6d, Hoop 2s, for H. Lower 6d, for Benmer's new house in Penzance New Borough 1s	9	0	
New house, Jo. Tremenheere	1	6	
The great Courtcledge, W. Maddren ..	2	0	
House in the old Borough, David Penlease ..		6	
Roscadgewell, H. Church	4	8	
Roskenwall, Sancreed, Bynards	1	10	
Brudany, Rich. Noye (Mousehole)		2	
Park Niolas	4	0	
Bolowan, Olyver Pindar..	2	6	
Roskestal, Jo. Roberts	2	0	
Aransawcth „	1	6	
W. Bainder	1	1	
Cranken in Maddern, Rich. Tom ..	1	3	
„ „ Tho. Cock	1	3	
Tho. Holla	1	2	
Boskenal ir. Buryan, Hugh Thomas ..	2	0	
Ragionnas (in Paul), W. Harry ..	3	6	
Trewen, J. Legar	1	7	
Pensance, Rich. Trevear	3	6	
Bruenny, Rich. Tremcarn		9½	
„ H. Hookin	1	4	
Polgoon, Jas. Jenkin	2	0	
Bowsava, Jo. Vibert		2	
Bologas Wartha, R. Mathew	4	0	
Trencre, widow Treneere	1 4	0	
Leddergwern, Geo. Veale	2	0	
Tresvenack, W. Badcock	1	4	
Goodale's house, Pensance, Margaret Hawes ..	1	6	
Tredavo		9	
„ Nich. Cock		6	
Troungle, W. Bodenar	2	2	
Pensance small tenures	4	10	
Kerismoor (in Paul)	3	4	
Tregenhog, W. Baynard	1	1	
Pensance new Borough, W. Maddern ..	1	0	
„ Tho. Pike	1	0	
Mousehole mill, Jo. Hutchens	8	0	
Chinose, Martin Eusback	2	6	
Trognseal and Kegwin, Jo. Bosvargo ..	2	3	
Divers free tenures, Tho. Tresilian.. ..	9	6	
Trendwenan, Jo. Lanyon	1	6	
Lagronsock, Jas. Penrose	1	0	
Firs, markets and quay duties of Pensance, Tho. Grosse mayor	1 0	0	
Several tenures, Tho. Treuren ..	·14	1½	
Treveneth, Rob. Binder	4	2	

		£	s.	d.
Three hemp gardens, Mousehole, Eliz. Wills ..		3	0	
One „ „ Jane Perrow..		1	6	
Several tenures in Paul and Mousehole, Martin Keigwin		6	4	
Hendra, Tho. Holber		4	8	
Penrose, W. John		1	0	
Higher Trembath, Pascoe Ellis			4	
Tresvenak, Edw. Tonken		5	2	
Polgoon, Tho. Tonken		2	0	
Bone, Geo. Bluett		1	3	
Trereen, Oliver John		2	1	

Conventionary Rents 1657.

		£	s.	d.
Tredavo, John Boos		5	0	0
„ W. Cotis		16	0	
„ Geo. Raw		12	0	
„ Geo. Jonas		10	0	
„ Martin Bramble		10	0	
Morhap, Tho. Grosse		12	0	
Barber's Acre 2s 6d, Morap Stick 1s 6d, meadow under the Morap 1s 8d, Jo. Fleming ..		5	8	
Park-an-Pound, Jo. Huchens	2	8	0
Park Cranken, widow Diggens		12	0
Little meadow under the Morap, Blanch Fenny		14	0
Kerris Vean, Arthur Berryman			
Pensance, Jo. Tresise		10	0
Penwolva, Rich. Tremcarne			
Barn and Mowhay, W. Hicks		4	0
Tredavo Down, Alex. Daniell	1	10	0

("Much omitted, especially in last list, I believe.")

Warrant to Arthur Paynter to officiate as Steward of the Manor of Alverton.

"These are to authorize you and I hereby do appoint you Steward of my Manor of Alverton in the county of Cornwall, to do and execute all and everything pertaining unto you as Steward thereof and to receive all Rents, arrerages of rents, Duties and Demands due or payable out of my said Manor and unto my use and to keep Court there for one whole year commencing from Lady-day last one thousand, six hundred, fifty and seven.

"Witness my hand and seal the thirtieth day of March 1657."

(Signed)   RICHARD DANIELL."

LANDS HELD IN 1873 BY PERSONS OF THE NAME OF BOASE.

From the Return of Owners of Land in England in 1873, presented to both Houses of Parliament. Lond., G. E. Eyre and W. Spottiswoode, 1875, 2 vols. fol.

					Annual Value.		
Name.	Place.	A.	R.	P.	£	s.	d.
Boase, Christopher	Zennor	15	0	34	6	10	0
„ F.	(St. Columb						
	Minor	111	1	11	106	0	0
„ Francis	Penzance	42	0	30	481	6	0
„ Henry	Dundee	1	2	0	115	0	0
„ John J. A.	Penzance	13	1	20	519	9	0
„ Wilmot	Zennor	15	0	35	7	0	0

INSCRIPTIONS ON SEPULCHRAL MONUMENTS.

In St. Mary's Church-yard, Penzance.

(1)

In this vault are deposited the remains of
Henry Boase, Esq.,
of this Town,
Who died on the 9th of April 1827, aged 63 years,
Leaving a wife and twelve children to deplore their loss.
He was a dutiful Son, an affectionate Husband, and a good
Father.
The Integrity and Liberality of his Social and Public
Character rendered him universally esteemed.
All the days of his life he walked in the fear of the Lord,
And he that giveth all things rewarded him abundantly.
On his deathbed he was calm and resigned, having a confident
hope of Salvation through the Redeemer's Atonement.

(2)

Life how short, eternity how long.
Sacred to the memory of Jane
daughter of John and Jane Boase
of this town who died Sunday April 28
1799 aged three years.
That life is long which answers life's great end.
Also of John their son
who departed this life on Sunday
March 6, 1808.

NOTE.—The above headstone was formerly the first on
the right hand as you entered at the North Gate, near the
top of the steps against the wall. It fell down in 1867 and
was completely destroyed.

(3)

Upper Surface—

Sacred
To the memory
of
Jane Boase,
Who died 12th Jan. 1821,
Aged 91 years.
Also of
Lieut. William Millett,
R.N.,
Who died the same day,
aged 58 years.
They were lovely and pleasant
in their lives,
And in death they were
not divided.   *(David.)*

West End—

In memory of
Jane Millett,
Widow of the late John Boase
Who died Feby. 16th 1861,
Aged 93 years.
May she rest in peace and
Awake to a joyful resurrection.

South Side—

In memory of
Three beloved children of
William Millet Boase and Jane Lydia his wife:
William Alfred, died June 1st 1839, aged 6 years.
Jane Lindsay, died March 18th 1841, aged 7 months.
Emily Wilmot, died April 25th 1842, aged 11 years.

They faded in the fair Spring time,
When bursting into bloom ;
All nature spoke of life and joy,
And nothing of the tomb.

But these new rising from the grave
With lustre brighter far shall shine,
Revive with never-ending life
The resurrection life divine.

North Side—

Sacred to the memory of
John Boase
Of Herbier House in this town,
Who died March 23rd 1850, aged 79 years.
Through a long life he was righteous in his conduct towards man
And devoted in his service to God,
By whose grace he was enabled to yield up his spirit
" In the sure and certain hope of a joyful resurrection,"
believing that " Those who sleep in Jesus,
God will bring with him." (i Thes. iv, 14.)

*East End—*Blank.

In Madron Church-yard.

John Jones Pearce
Born April 15th 1795 :
Died July 10th 1833.

In the Penzance Cemetery.

(1)

Charlotte Boase born Oct. 30 1802 Died Sept 10 1873.

(2)

In memory of
Charles Sholl who died Nov. 29, 1870,
Aged 75 Years.
Truth was his guide.

In Manaccan Church.

In memory of
Robert Horatio
Son of Charles Sholl, Esq.,
Collector of Customs at the Port of Gweek,
who died Treath 8th July 1845,
Aged 16 years.
Some of his last words to his sorrowing friends were
" You weep, but I rejoice."

In Kenwyn Churchyard.

(1)

Sacred to the memory of
William Sholl, Gent.,
of
Condura in St. Clements
Who died Dec. 20th 1801,
Aged 67 years.
Also
Cecilia
Daughter of the above,
Aged 15 years.

(2)

Richard Sholl
Departed this life
January 30th 1844,
Aged 77.
Anna Maria
his wife
departed this life
Nov. 30th 1842,
Aged 76,
Also Jane
daughter of the above who died
April 22nd 1859,
Aged 59.

In St. Leonard's Churchyard, Exeter.

Here rests
Sarah Anne Sholl,
Born 23rd February 1833,
Died 8th September 1857.

In Plymouth Cemetery.

Anne Naomi Boase
Died Feby. 9th 1874,
Aged 71 years.
Blessed are the dead, which die in the Lord.

In St. George's Churchyard, Tiverton.

" In a vault beneath are deposited the remains of
Ann Boase
And
Jane Mary Boase
In memory of whom this stone is erected by their
affectionate parents.
The former died the 1st day of December 1804, aged 6
years. The latter departed this life the 11th day of March
1822 in the 26th year of her age.
Also of Arthur Boase, Father of the above, who departed
this life Sept. 10, 1829
Aged 72 years.
Also of Hannah Boase his widow, who died Feby. 21, 1848
Aged 84 years."

In the Parish Churchyard at Albury, Surrey.

In memory of
Charles William Boase.
Born in London 8th June 1804,
Died at Albury 7th June 1872.

" Weeping may endure for a night
But joy cometh in the morning."

In the Cemetery, Constitution Road, Dundee.

In his favour is life:
Weeping
May endure for a night
But joy
Cometh in the morning.

In
Memory
of
Helen
Daughter of
Charles W. Boase
Banker, Dundee
And Helen his wife,
Who was born 22 June 1836,
And died 28th Sep. 1838.

Also of
Charles W. Henry
their son,
Who was born 1st Nov. 1833
And died 26th Decr. 1838.

Also of
Edith Lindsay
their daughter,
Who was born 4th June 1840,
And died
1st March 1841.

In
Memory also
Of the aforesaid
Charles W. Boase
Who was born in London
8th June 1804,
Resided 50 years in Dundee
And departed this life
7th June 1872
At Albury in Surrey,
And is buried in the
Churchyard there.

In the Eastern Necropolis, Dundee.

(1)
In memory of
Anna Maria,
The beloved wife of
Alfred W. Pearce, Dundee,
And their daughter
Anna Henrietta.

(2)
Erected
by
Alfred Boase
and
Ellen Bradley Boase
In memory of their daughter
Alice Marion,
Who died 28th Feby. 1872,
Aged two years and eleven months.
I look for the resurrection of the dead.

In Kensal-Green Cemetery.

I.H.S.
" Blessed are the dead that die in the Lord."
Rosanna,
The beloved wife of John Symes, Esqr.,
Died June 26th 1856,
Aged 42 years.
The above named
John Symes
Died January 15th 1873,
Aged 62 years.

NOTES AND CORRECTIONS.

In Pedigree Sheet—

John of Tredavo, according to one account, 'died about 1680, leaving one son.'

Robert bur. 172? is thought to have also had a dau. Mary, who m. † 24 Dec. 1728 William Richards, by licence, both of Penzance.

Richard senior, according to one account, 'm. Bodinnar of Burian.'

Phillis wife of William Eyre, farmer, d. at her brother's residence, Pendennis Castle, 2 Sep. 1844, aged 64. Jane Rawe her niece was present: her brother John Boase was barrack master at Pendennis.

Jane dau. of John Boase by Jane Millett was b. 1796, d. Sunday 28 Apl. 1799; her brother John d. Sunday 6 March 1808.

Arthur of Madron m. Jane Lugg, 'witnesses William Pollard, Francis Paull.'

Richard of Gulval was also of Trythall in Madron, and buried on the south side of Madron churchyard, but the monu. is now sunk and covered by the soil.

Jane, dau. of Richard of Gulval, bap. 1798, d. ca. 1820.

Harriet, dau. of Richard of Gulval, bap. ‖ 30 Nov. 1801.

Jane Mary m. Hoskin of Camelford, and had by him William, Henry, Mary, and two other sons and a daughter.

John m. Jane Millett † (not ‖).

Elizabeth Valentina wife of H. S. Boase d. Scafield house, 5 Magdalen place, Dundee, 13 May 1876 at 5.30 a.m., bur. N.W. corner of Western cemetery, Dundee, 18 May.

Charles William m. ‡ 8 June 1804, bap. 26 July, m. Helen dau of William Lindsay by Alicia Mackenzie.

John m. Elizabeth Harvey, was m. at Burian by Richard Pearce, curate.

Rosanna m. Symes, and d. Thursday 26 June 1856. Her husband also was buried at Kensal Green.

Charles William Henry b. 1 Nov. 1833, d. ¶ 26 Dec. 1838.

Alice Anne m. Jevon James Muschamp Perry.

Helen b. 22 June 1836, d. 28 Sep. 1838.

Edward b. §16 Dec. 1841, m. 31 Oct. 1871 Emilia.

John b. ‡ 4 Nov. 1837.

Charlotte Anne m. R. M. Tweedy ‖ 22 July 1863.

Robert Richards son of Henry Boase b. 14 Oct. 1857.

Text—

Col. 1. The following curious early notice of the name of Boase occurs in Hector Boethius' *History of Scotland*, lib. 12, Fol. 266, line 65 (ed. Paris, 1527.) After speaking of the families which came over with Queen Margaret from Hungary, he adds:—" Other families came over at different times from France, as Frascir, Sinclair, Bosual, Montalth, Montgomerie, Cambell, Bons, Betuin, Taillefer, Bodenal." The author of *The Norman People*, 1874, derives the name Bowes from Hugh de Boves (from Boves in Picardy), King John's Admiral, who perished in the great storm 26 Sep. 1215. (See Rymer's Foedera, i, 134, Rot. Pat. i, 144, Wendover, iii, 287.) This is merely conjecture. John however did give lands near Penzance to another of his chiefs, Henry le Tyes (Teutonicus), a military engineer from Germany.

Col. 1. Blanch Shutford, bur. * 4 Nov. 1722.

Col. 1. John Bremble had a son John bap. * 1 May 1706,

who m. Cecilia, and had by her John bap. ' 8 Jan. 174?.

Col. 3. John Rowe's son by Elizabeth Harvey Boase, also called John, b. Carhayes 28 Jan. 1811, now living at Frognal House, Hampstead, m. Mary Ann dau. of John May Andrew of Tregarden, widow of William Warne b. 26 May 1812. (See Sir J. Maclean, ii, 530.) It was this son who took out the patents.

Col. 4. John Hewett published a new edition of Carew's *Cornwall* in 1769. In the Madron register we find :— '1754 Nov. 20. John Hewett m. Jane Adams, both of Penzance.' H. Boase adds:—'The monthly publications did not reach us at soonest before the fifteenth of the month : there was no coach westward of Exeter, the mail which was forwarded thence to Penzance three times a week on horseback was in all five days coming from London. But even then the change which had taken place within the memory of aged people was thought wonderful. At the beginning of the last century only one newspaper, and that once a-week, reached as far as Godolphin, whither it was sent by the Lord Treasurer Godolphin, and laid on the table of the Great Hall for the accommodation of the gentlemen of the district, who rode over occasionally to learn the news.'

Col. 7, line 9. She m. (3) Mr. Gilson.

Col. 7. H. Boase's house was at first called Prospect Place.

Col. 8. The arms are wrongly described. Read :— " Argent, on a chevron engrailed Azure (between two Cornish choughs wings elevated proper in chief, and an anchor erect in base Sable) five bezants; and for crest on a wreath of the colours, a demi-lion Sable sem c of bezants and mullets Or, alternate, holding between the paws a sheaf of five arrows, barbed and flighted proper, banded Gules.

Col. 9. H. S. Boase on leaving Penzance received a testimonial of a silver salver from the members of the Royal Cornwall Geological Society.

Col. 9. Read : ' Turnbull and Co.'

Col. 9, line 17 from bottom. Read : ' He erected the Wellfield Works.'

Col. 9, line 8 from bottom. Read : ' Miss Elizabeth Richards.'

Col. 10. Arthur Boase was trained in the mechanic's shop of Messrs. Baxter Brothers and Co.

Col. 11. J. J. A. Boase and Charlotte Sholl m. by Rev. Francis Jenkins.

Col. 12. C. W. Boase wrote the articles on Cornish Saints in Smith's *Dictionary of Christian Biography, Literature, and Doctrines*, 1876.

Col. 18, line 35. Read : Manager of the Bank 1 Apl. 1829.

Col. 14. Edward Boase saw service in the North-West of India with the 93rd Highlanders.

Col. 15. G. C. Boase bap. by J. Ouseby chaplain of the Lock Hospital. At the age of eight and a half, he was placed under the care of William Whitehead, curate of Mylor. W M. Boase his cousin was also educated by Rev. W. Whitehead, when the latter was curate of St. Keverne.

Col. 18. Tonken Boase and John Fenny leased the Market and Quay dues at Penzance in 1659.

Touken Boase had a seat in Penzance Church 1674 ;
as also had Susan Boase, probably a relation.
Col. 20.   Charles Boase d. 1873, bur. cemetery, Ply-
mouth, where is his monument.
Francis Boase, Mayor 1859, 1864, 1866-7, 1870, 1873.
Col. 22.   John Boase, ? bur. † 21 Sep. 1706, mar. † 31
July 1768, Elizabeth Lawrence of Madron, ? bur. ‖ 12
May 1793.
Col. 24.   Is the name Lucretiá *French*, connected with
that of Rawlen Boase *Gallicus*. Was she his daughter ?
Col. 24.   Wife of Arthur Boase d. Lamerton 20 Sep.
1871, age 52.
Col. 24.   Mrs. Ann Boase, formerly Miss Betty of St.
Austell, m. Daylesford, Victoria, Australia, 17 June
1869 Thomas Garmon.
Col. 25.   Ralph Beard's farthing token reads (see *Journal
of Royal Inst., of Cornwall*, No. xvi. 1874, p. 41.)
      O.   Ralph Beard—A mullet.
      R.   In Penzance 1667—A mullet.
Ralph and his wife Dorothy both had seats in Penzance
Church, 1674.
Col. 26, line 18 from bottom, m. Ann eld. dau. of Thomas
and Cordelia Husband, d. Meare 1866, aged 82.
Col. 28.   Thomas Glason m. Elizabeth 2 dau. of John
Levelis, ? 1600.
John Glasson m. Beatrix d. of John Rosewhorne, ? 1590.
John Glasson m. † 20 June 1646, Maud
Christopher Glasan m. † 3 Oct. 1646, Prudence
Alice wife of Christopher Glasan bur. † 25 July 1646.
Christopher Glasan bur. † 10 July 1654.
Prudence widow of Christopher Glasan bur. † 7 Dec.
1656.
James Glasson m. Jane 3 dau. of Thomas Hosking of
Landithy, ? 1760
George Glasson of Madron m. † 9 July 1754 Eleanor
Kneebone of Madron, witness John Glasson.
John son of George Glasson bap. † 11 July 1756.
Thomas Glasson of Gulval m. † 27 March 1772, Phillis
Argall, of Madron, witnesses Joseph Glasson, Richard
Vingoe.
1826, July 4, Lieut. Glasson, R.M., m. at Newington,
Cecilia only surviving dau. of late Sir John Mouat-
Keith, Bart., and sister of Capt. Sir Geo. Mouat-
Keith, Bart., R.N.
1852, Sep. 8, Henry Glasson of St. John's Cambridge,
m. at Falmouth, Lucy 1 dau. of Lieut. T. A. Lewis,
R.N. Ponwenock, Falmouth.
Col. 29.   (1) Ann m. Nicholas Wallis. See Wallis pedigree
col. 56.
(2) Christopher, bur. † 16 Oct. 1742, in 20th year unm.
Richard Hosking of Lelant, d. circa 1869, leaving a
son, the Rev. Henry Hosking.
Mary dau. of James Hosking was bur. Gulval, 5 Dec.
1795.
Final agreement 7 George III, 'from the day of the
Holy Trinity, in three weeks,' between William
Ustick petitioner and George Ley and Catherine his
wife deforciants, of 4 messuages, 4 gardens, 5 orchards,
40 acres of land, 15 acres of meadow, 30 acres of
pasture, and 20 acres of moor, in Lariggan, otherwise
Lariggan Wartha and Lariggan Woollas : George
and Catherine warrant to William, who gives them
£160.
Col. 29.   1 Aug. 1767. George Ley to William Usticke of
Nanee Alvern. Deed to levy a fine and lead the uses.
Lariggan then occupied by George Ley, Richard
Treeve, Henry Hick, Francis Boase and others.
George Ley also held the Hay meadows, the old
Bowling Green, and the new Bowling Green in
Penzance then occupied by George Ley and Andrew
Stone. Reference is made to a previous deed of the
Daniel family, viz. :—

5 Apl. 1649.   Alexander Daniel to William first son of
Sir George Whitmore and Ralph Durante : Marriage
settlement of Richard Daniel with Elizabeth Dalley,
d. of Thomas Dalley, late haberdasher of London
deceased, and of Isabel his late wife, now the wife of
the said Raphe Durant : lands in manor of Allwarton
and Pensannce late parcel of the possessions of Henry
late Earl of Rutland ... and those two Laregans ....
and William Madderne's curtelago . , and lands in
St. German's, Truroe, Kenwyne, Clements : Grace
now wife of Alexander Daniel is mentioned.
Will of George Ley of Penzance, 12 Aug. 1767. I gave
on my marriage with Catherine, a bond for £360 for
her use if she survived me. I now give her instead
an annuity of £20 : to my second and third sons
George and John and to my daughter Catherine £200
each on their severally attaining 21 : to Thomas
Saunders Allen of St. Just in Penwith, gentleman,
and Joseph Beard of Penzance, pewterer, my lands in
trust for my eldest son Daniel for his use on attaining
21.   Witnesses D. Dennis, John Beard junr., Thomas
Hacker.   Proved 20 Dec. 1776 before Edward
Pavell, clerk M.A., surrogate, and administration to
Daniel Ley being of age.
Will of Daniel Ley of Penzance, 19 Sep. 1806. I give
to my sister Catherine Ley £50, and a life annuity of
£30 as rent-charge on Lariggan : to Margery Pascoe
of Penzance £10 10s. : to Arthur Daniel jun., son of
Arthur Daniel of Penzance, if he outlive my wife
Alice, a life annuity of £8 on Lariggan : to my
servant Elizabeth Barnes £10 : Lariggan and the
Wastrell or common called The Green (extending
from the West hedge of the road leading from the
Green to Lariggan, called Lariggan Lane, to the East
end of fields lying under the Chapel yard of Penzance,
called Close Years, now the lands of Richard
Oxnam, merchant) to pay these annuities to John
Batten jun., merchant, and John Giddy, surgeon, in
trust for Catherine Ley's children ; then (1) one half
for my cousin Jonah Milford jun., son of Jonah
Milford of Truro, and his children, then for my
cousin Samuel Milford, another son of Jonah senior,
then to the right heirs of Daniel Ley for ever ; (2)
the other half to my kinsman John Beard of Penzance, then to Lucy wife of John Beard, and after
their lives to their children, then to the right heirs of
Daniel Ley.   Alice Ley to be executrix and residuary
legatee.   Witnesses James Pascoe, R. H. Bodilly,
William Stevens.   Proved in Prerogative Court of
Canterbury 29 Jan. 1807.
Col. 30.   Robert Luke was named Alderman of Penzance
in the charter of 1614.
Col. 31.   Stephen Luke, and William Luke's wife, and
the widow Luke had seats in Penzance Church 1674.
Col. 32.   Samuel Milford of Truro m. Ann Jenkin of this
parish 12 March 1804 : by me Samuel Gurney, curate :
witnesses Elizabeth Chester, Henry Milford, Grace
Jenkin, Thomas P. Ashwin. (Redruth register.)
Col. 32.   1. Tonale Milford, d. 4 Sep. 1825.
Col. 32.   On 23 day of fifth month 1808 was born in
Truro to Samuel Milford and Ann his wife a son
named Henry C., witnesses John Buckingham, surgeon,
Mary Beard Sholl. (Certificate.)
Col. 34, line 25 from bottom. Dele (? 29).
Col. 35.   Richard Oxnam was Lieut.-Col. Commandant
of Third or Mounts Bay Regiment of Local Militia.
Col. 35, line 9.   Died 1793, aged 63.
Col. 35.   Mary Oxenham Oddy d. Victoria place, Pen-
zance, 17 May 1876 in her 73rd year.
Col. 35.   Rev. W. Oxenham, ? bap. ‖ 2 Dec. 1771.
Col. 35.   Mary Elizabeth b. Paul 23 Feb.

Col. 38. William Pearce was Mayor of Penzance 1683, and with his wife Elizabeth had seats in the church 1674.

Col. 38. Richard Pearce was Mayor 1689, 1694.

Col. 38. John Jones Pearce was Captain and Adjutant of Third or Mounts Bay Regiment of Local Militia. He was Mayor of Penzance 1820, 1822.

Col. 38. Richard of Tredinny, curate of Gulval 1754.

Col. 39. Richard, Mayor 1837, 1842, 1847, 1851, 1858.

Col. 41. John Perys, Vicar of S. Erth 29 Apl. 1533, d. within a few months.

Col. 42. Thomas Pears had seat in Penzance church 1674.

Col. 43. Michael Pearce occurs in G. H. Millett's 'Penzance, Past and Present' p. 43.

Col. 44. (1) Anthony m. Petronilla dau. of James Chidleigh.

Col. 44, line 5, Trewarveoith Marchas.

Col. 44. (3) Margaret m. William Cruwys of Chulmleigh

Col. 44. Dele (5) Thomas, (6) James.

Col. 45. Martin Richards and his wife, and Nicholas Richards had seats in Penzance church 1674 : Nicholas Richards and Nehemiah Batten leased the market and quay dues of Penzance in 1794 at £240 10s., and £309 19s. respectively.

Col. 45. (1) Robert, ? bur. 13 Oct 1765.

Col. 45. (2) Richard of Bosvigo bapt. 26 Jan. 173½, bur. 30 Mch, 1781. m. Eleanor dau. of Dunstan of Kea, bur. 25 Dec. 1811.

Col. 45. 1. Richard d. 30 Jan. 1844, aged 77. His wife d. 30 Nov. 1842.

Col. 45. iv. James, ? bap. 14 June 1795.

Col. 45. ii. Jane d. 22 Apl. 1859, age 59.

iv. Emma m. 29 Apl. 1822.

Another dau, Betsy was bur. 22 June 1787.

b. William, ? m. Elizabeth, and had a dau. Mary Lavin.

Col. 46. v. James m. 1831 : he was perhaps previously married, as a James was bur. 21 Aug. 1831, aged 2. His other children may have been, James bur. 25 May 1841, aged 6, from Calenick St.; and Anna Maria bur. 17 Dec. 1834, aged 2, from Castle St.

Col. 46. ii. Louisa Teresa d. 1864.

For Rauceley read Rauceby.

Read : M. S. C. S.

Mary Luke of Kenwyn was related to Joseph Ferris and to Vibert of Penzance.

2 lines from end. Read ; 1787.

Col. 47. Robert second son of Augustus Sholl of Truro d. London 21 Jan, 1828.

Col. 47. Charles William Sholl's wife d. in Tennessee, U.S. America, 1864.

Col. 47. iv. Robert, see Fitzroy, 'Voyage of Adventurer and Beagle' I pp. 23, 24, 65, 121.

Col. 48. 4. Elizabeth, by one account d. unm. at Bath.

(1). Mary Sholl bap. 27 Jan. 173½

ADDENDA.

In St. Mary's Church Yard, Penzance.

North Side.

In this vault are deposited the remains of
Henry Boase, Esq.
[See ante Col. 59.]

South Side.

Within this tomb
By the side of her husband's remains,
After a widowed separation of 36 years,
Reposes the body of
Anne Craig,
Wife of the late Henry Boase of Penzance,
Who departed this life on the 7th February 1863,
In her 88th year.

Ten surviving children
Hold in affectionate remembrance
Her motherly care and personal worth,
And looking forward in faith as she did to the resurrection
of the dead,
They humbly hope for a joyful reunion
Through the merits of our Lord and Saviour
Jesus Christ.

Top.

In this vault
Are also deposited the remains of
Alfred,
The youngest son of Henry Boase, Esq.,
Who died at Bodmin 19th Feb. 1829,
Aged 16 years.

Also the remains of
Jessy Anne,
The daughter of
Mitchel Thomson, Surgeon R.N.,
and
Of Grace Lucilla daughter of
the late Henry Boase, Esq.,
Who died the 16th October 1845,
Aged 3½ years.
Of such is the kingdom of heaven.—Matthew, chap. xix.

In Chatham Churchyard.

Sacred to the memory of Richard Sholl, Esq., R.N., who after serving his country 35 years in various parts of the globe, departed this life December 17, 1836, in the fifty-first year of his age, being then Purser of the Ordinary at Chatham. His excellency as an officer is testified by all with whom he sailed, his warm and generous affection for his family by their deep regret at his loss, and his worth as a friend by all that knew him. *Requiescat in pace.*

NOTE.

Mabel daughter of Lewis Charles and Julia Thomson was born at 14 Seaton Terrace, Mutley, Plymouth, 5 June 1876 at 5.45 p.m.